R/T

Mothermania

Mothermania

A Psychological Study of Mother-Daughter Conflict

Jane B. Abramson, Ph.D.

Lexington Books
D.C. Heath and Company/Lexington, Massachusetts/Toronto

Library of Congress Cataloging-in-Publication Data

Abramson, Jane B.
  Mothermania: a psychological study of mother-daughter conflict.

  Bibliography: p.
  Includes index.
  1. Women—United States—Psychology.
2. Mothers and daughters—United States.
3. Interpersonal relations.   4. Self-actualization
(Psychology).   I. Title.
HQ1206.A22   1987   306.8'743   85-45520
ISBN 0-669-11930-X (alk. paper)

Published simultaneously in Canada
Printed in the United States of America
Casebound International Standard Book Number: 0-669-11930-X
Library of Congress Catalog Card Number: 85-45520

The paper used in this publication meets the minimum requirements
of American National Standard for Information Sciences—
Permanence of Paper for Printed Library Materials,
ANSI Z39.48-1984.
∞ ™

87   88   89   90   91   8   7   6   5   4   3   2   1

No Freudian trauma or loss of a loved one is as
devastating to the human spirit as some
prolonged ambivalent relationships that leave
us forever unable to say goodbye.

—*George E. Vaillant*

To the doctor who helped me know my child.

Contents

Figures and Tables

Figures

Tables

Preface

While I am aware of the limits to which the findings presented in this book can be generalized, I also have confidence that much can be learned from a well-studied sample such as the one discussed here. Only now are we beginning to find out what happens in the intrapsychic life of women after menopause.

In formulating my research and my conclusions about the results, I relied on common sense and on my clinical experience, as well as on the findings of other researchers in female psychology. The work of predecessors suggested many important questions for exploration. Nevertheless, some of my findings may prove wrong. Certainly, replication of them with other populations, which I hope to see occur, would increase my confidence in their wider applicability, to women in other cultures, for example, or to women of other age groups.

In advance of such confirmation, I am convinced that the results of this study—and the experiences of my older subjects—are relevant for women today. In spite of their individual differences, the women in my study shared certain experiences as part of a particular age group moving through time. Their common survival of the Depression profoundly affected their attitudes toward work and financial security. Their experiences and expectations, though sharply different from those of today's young and even middle-aged women, are replete with intergenerational lessons.

Younger women can learn from the stories of these older women how their lives were molded by choices that they made or failed to make. In their stories we see that while the range of choices available to women may have multiplied exponentially in recent years, earlier generations of women also exercised important options. In fact, we see that the study women were sometimes held back less by lack of opportunity than by personal limitations and/or by their own senses of personal limitation. They had more choices than they realized.

One finding that transcends generational differences relates to the meaning of motherhood: the older women studied displayed wide variations in maturity level, or separateness from their own mothers, despite the homogeneity of the sample and the fact that all had been mothers. Their ability to use the mothering experience for their own growth depended on their prior histories, especially on the kind of mothering they had themselves received.

So it seems that some things never change. While child-raising practices may alter as each succeeding generation of parents attempts to surpass its predecessors in perfect parenting, underlying maternal feelings and attitudes retain their transcending significance. There is nothing new and nothing old-fashioned about the impact on development caused by the mother's feelings toward her child (though we now know that they may be a function of her own mother's feelings about her!).

Other findings may apply across the board: No one pattern or life-style ensured well-being in later life. Traditional developmental tasks such as needing to establish an independent self were no different for women who entered adulthood before the expansion of work and career opportunities for women. Women may define themselves differently today in terms of their work roles, but the pull in the opposite direction, to merge blissfully and symbiotically with the mother is as strong as ever. It is inherent in the human condition.

Separation from the mother is scary business.

Acknowledgments

I t is difficult to put into words my deep feeling of affection and appreciation for the many people who have helped me during the past three years of research and writing. My sincerest thanks go to the women who were so candid about revealing themselves to me in the hope that others might learn something of enduring value about mothering and loving from their experiences. To them I owe a debt of gratitude.

Not unlike other journeys into the self, the process of telling their stories has been both painful and rewarding. It proved to be impossible to write about these women's pain and longing without touching off resonant chords in my own experience. I necessarily made contact with the most vulnerable parts of myself, and like Marie and Rachel, whom you will meet shortly, emerged a very different person. Thus, my parallel adventure with them into the "unknown and unknowable" has enriched my life and expanded my possibilities. (In preparing this book, I have also drawn heavily on my personal psychoanalysis. With all its shortcomings, I believe that the analytic perspective offers the deepest insights into what it means to be fully human, and why we behave as we do.)

In order to protect the privacy of the women in the study, I have made minor changes, as far as identifying details are concerned, using fictitious names, geographical locations, husband's occupation, family business, and so forth. Therefore, the case studies are factual for the most part, except for such revealing information.

During the period of research and writing, I had my own support system. One person in particular who merits a special kind of tribute is my talented editor and friend, Miriam Raskin, who helped me in translating esoteric psychological concepts into everyday language. Reaching individuals outside the academic community was an important goal of mine. In addition, my sincerest thanks go to Grace Baruch, a developmental psychologist who helped in the early stages of this project and to two valued friends, Jackie Dukker and Hollis Sigler, who contributed their artistic ideas which do so much to enhance this work. I cannot thank them enough.

There are other people who have influenced me greatly, but whose influence was not confined to the writing of this book. They include my parents, Sam and Helen Beber, who believed in me; my children, Anne, Paul, Amy, and Rachel, who endured many a lapse in mothering; and especially my husband Floyd, whose advice, insights, and loving concern were always "optimally available," unlike those of even the best of mothers. Because of them this book is about love.

Mothermania

1
Putting Motherhood to the Test

Psychologists have been somewhat slower than other professional observers in responding to the aging of America. The relative scarcity of serious work in this ever more important area derives from the long-standing bias within the profession toward viewing childhood as the quintessentially formative phase. Significant psychological changes are assumed to occur almost exclusively in the early years, while adulthood is seen as a relatively static elaboration of childhood events.

There are, therefore, few useful hypotheses and even fewer useful tools for evaluating what hypotheses there are about psychological processes in adults. While provocative theories have been advanced by the exceptional psychoanalysts who have written about adult issues, there has been little clinical evidence to consider. It was with the hope of adding a drop to the nearly empty bucket of available research that I undertook a study of the psychological adaptations of chronologically mature women to the deaths of their mothers.

My interest had been piqued by the suggestion made by several writers that important issues, unresolved in childhood, can actually be reapproached and resolved during milestone events in adulthood. Becoming a parent is such a milestone event, one in which the new parent gains an opportunity to rework childhood conflicts from the other side of the fence.

To at least one theorist in this field, motherhood offers the most likely biological route to psychological maturity,[1] while another suggests that women who have and raise children receive personal validation through their children that helps them—the mothers—become more complete and separate persons.[2] These contentions led me to hypothesize that the psychological benefits attributed to motherhood should reveal themselves in times of loss. If mothering truly enables women to rework residual separation issues to satisfactory resolution, women who have and raise children should be able to accept the deaths of their own mothers with equanimity (because maternal loss is prototypic of all losses one experiences).

This line of thinking breaks with traditional object relations theory, which holds early relationship experiences to be most influential in determining the eventual life patterns of ordinary people. Accordingly, how a child relates to early "objects" (a term that, in psychoanalytic jargon, refers to parents or parent substitutes) largely sets the pattern for all subsequent relationships, although some allowance is generally made for modification of basic relationship paradigms during the course of development.

The speculation that motherhood in and of itself might act to modify early relationship patterns contains the seed of more than passing interest to many women who are or contemplate being mothers. It raises question after question. Is motherhood per se good for the mental health of women? Are early relationship problems ameliorated or exacerbated when the child becomes the mother? Are women who have and raise children really better able to handle the inevitable losses that occur in later years, especially the deaths of their own mothers, than women who have not had children?

For the purposes of my research, the proliferating questions were distilled into one: Does the fact that a woman becomes a mother by and large override early developmental deficits (such as failure to resolve separation) or are these early deficits deep enough that they continue to determine experience throughout life, regardless of the milestones passed along the way? The search for answers focused on thirty-nine women who had borne and raised children, had passed the age of sixty, and had sustained the losses of their mothers.

To my everlasting pleasure, this small study and the new scale developed for it managed to produce findings that, at the least, indicate the need for more and deeper mining of the source. The carefully studied results suggest strongly that the view of motherhood as the exclusive route to emotional maturity for women may be unfounded and that women may, in fact, put their self-esteem in jeopardy by neglecting those aspects of their lives that relate to acquiring competence in the work place. These findings, while hardly startling, should come as happy news to the thousands of women who have made their own life decisions on the basis of consonance between inner and outer reality.

A little more startling was the revelation that the study subjects with the most favorable outcomes (the healthiest women emotionally, based on their overall high functioning scores) were very maternal, sensitive individuals who value personal feelings and relationships. The most "successful" women studied had found their way through the conflicting values of our time to an integrated worldview that works for them. How much of the underlying ability to function optimally was determined in childhood, how much in mothering?

But elaboration of the findings must await at least a superficial consideration of the study's theoretical underpinnings.

Notes

1. Therese Benedek, in Henri Parens, "Parenthood as a Developmental Phase," panel report, *Journal of the American Psychoanalytic Association* 23(1975):475–96.

2. Judith W. Ballou, *The Influence of Object-Relational Paradigms on the Experience of Pregnancy and Early Motherhood* (Ann Arbor, Mich.: University Microfilms, 1975).

2
Not Just Another Beautiful Phase

Y ears after Sigmund Freud divided childhood into the biologically based psychosexual stages, knowledge of which has become part of chic culture, Margaret S. Mahler made a noteworthy addition to the psychoanalytic understanding of infantile development that has not yet penetrated the public consciousness. For every person who can assess the anal and oral fixations of an associate in the way of cocktail party banter, how many are prepared to comment on their own rapprochement crises? Although Mahler's theory of the separation-individuation process had a profound effect on the contemporary psychoanalytic view of early childhood development, it has simply failed, thus far, to attract the popular attention that it deserves.

Yet behind the almost intentionally esoteric terms (which will be explained in a moment) lie important truths. In a time when women are becoming increasingly conscious of their own needs and possibilities, the system developed by this psychoanalytic theorist provides a useful frame of reference for heightened understanding not only of the children that women bear, but also of the children that those women were and of the adults that they more or less had to become. And despite the forbidding aspects of the terminology attached to it, the theory itself is clear and accessible.

Separation is universal and primal but not at first conscious. Physical separation from the mother precedes psychological awareness of the separation; we are all born unconscious of our separateness and must all come to terms with it if we are to live independent lives. The process that infants undergo while discovering and developing their separate identities is what Mahler termed *separation-individuation*, combining into one useful heading the reciprocal actions of tearing away from the mother and becoming a unique individual. *Individuation* itself refers to the process first identified by Jung as the gradual development of a unified, integrated personality.

So the separation-individuation task involves the young child's initial awareness of the difference between itself and everything else that is not itself; the first tentative moves toward developing its own individual, individuated, characteristics; and, perhaps most significantly, the first efforts to establish autonomy vis-à-vis the parental figure. The degree to which that autonomy and a consequent sense of self are achieved at this very early stage is believed to have profound implications for later life.

Mahler views the separation-individuation process as a vital phase of the developmental continuum that takes the child from birth to the achievement of selfhood. Two earlier phases of infant development pave the way. The most primitive, objectless phase, which Mahler terms *autistic*, categorizes the newborn infant, so incapable of contact with others that it is unaware and indifferent to parents and others. In the second phase, *symbiosis*, the bond between mother and child is renewed; the two are again as one so that the infant recaptures the security of the womb.

Self-discovery occurs in the separation-individuation phase that follows, a phase so crucial that Mahler established four discrete subphases to describe its characteristic events.

The first sign of demarcation of self from the mother occurs in the first subphase, *differentiation*; incipient self-awareness is marked by the infant's smile in the presence of the mother. In the second subphase, *practicing*, the child tries out new skills while becoming temporarily oblivious to the mother. In the fourth and most advanced subphase, which Mahler calls *on-the-way-to-object constancy*, the child approaches a stable sense of self vis-à-vis the parent figure and is "on the way" to complete separation. This is as far as anyone can go; complete separation is, in Mahler's view, only theoretically possible.

It is the third subphase that is the most relevant to the present context. Mahler uses the term *rapprochement* (usually pronounced as if it were not French, as if there were an English word like "reapproachment," which would be entirely apt for this purpose) to describe the stage in which the child gives up a temporary unconcern about the mother's presence and expresses clear desires to have the mother share every new experience. The new active approach behavior is, however, mixed with signs of rebellion as the child begins its struggle for autonomy.

Ambivalence is the hallmark of the rapprochement phase. Mahler describes it as a period of "oscillation between the longing to merge blissfully with the good object representation, with the erstwhile (in one's fantasy, at least) 'all good' symbiotic mother, and the defense against re-engulfment by her, which could cause loss of autonomous self-identity."[1]

How well the child moves through this stage depends, somewhat paradoxically, on the success achieved in previous stages. If there has been optimal symbiosis, the child will move away from the mother gradually and will undergo a relatively painless separation into the practicing phase. If all goes well, the end of the practicing phase (age ten to eighteen months) has the child confidently returning to its mother after making increasingly longer independent forays.

Rapprochement, which lasts from about fourteen months of age to twenty-four months and beyond, is marked by the child's recognition of the mother as a separate individual to whom it returns after "practicing" independent experiences. With a short-lived illusion of omnipotence, the toddler takes pleasure in sharing experiences and possessions with the mother. "Curiously," says Mahler, "it is precisely at this moment, when he is at the peak of his powers that his narcissism is most in danger of deflation."[2]

What happens is that the child becomes so aware of its own separateness and relative insignificance that it can no longer maintain its feeling of omnipotence. It gradually recognizes its separateness from its parents, who have interests of their own to pursue. Unable to satisfy all its needs for itself, the child is torn between simultaneous and mutually exclusive wishes to be autonomous and to be a baby, and clings to the mother while rejecting her at the same time.

Mahler identified the moment of most acute realization of separateness as a critical subphase, a rapprochement crisis that threatens the child's new faith in its own power. Typically, the toddler reacts by doing what it can to make its environment conform to earlier, more comfortable perceptions, which is naturally impossible. Mahler observed and meticulously described the toddler's resulting ambivalence to its mother that is demonstrated through temper tantrums, whining, and sadness.

But despite the inner tensions created by the rapprochement crisis, Mahler's case studies showed that normal children were generally able to get their needs fulfilled by the mother, sometimes against substantial odds.[3] Mahler eventually noted that "the emotional growth of the mother, her willingness to let go . . . to give . . . as the mother bird does, a gentle push" is an important factor in the pursuit of healthy individuation.[4] Although she viewed separation as a lifelong process, for the course of her study, Mahler's emphasis was on the child's intrapsychic processes.

Her observation that children seemed able to find fulfillment of their needs did not, as far as Mahler was concerned, minimize the effort involved in dealing with the painful losses and longings of the rapprochement crisis. Indeed, she described the separation process as a harrowing struggle from which even "the most normally endowed child with the most optimally available mother" cannot survive unscathed.[5] Everyone, therefore, suffers from ego wounds sustained in the battle for separation-individuation. Avoiding the struggle is no solution; failure to separate appropriately during this early phase simply prolongs the quest for personal autonomy. Fixation at the rapprochement level is seen as being at the root of the most pervasive anxiety among those seeking professional help, according to Mahler.

Whether or not they are satisfactorily resolved in childhood, the ambivalences of the separation struggle are echoed in later life when the child who has become a woman faces serial separations: in broken engagements or severed marriages; in the maturing of her children as they go off to kindergarten, grow independent, move out of the nest; and the ultimate separations, the deaths of loved ones. Other theorists have postulated that unresolved conflicts that develop around the separation-individuation task are renewed when such losses are experienced and that the reactivation provides an opportunity for amelioration of the conflict by that individual.

If later losses are likely to reawaken unresolved separation conflicts, none is more likely to do so than the loss of the original partner in the primal separation drama. Like the toddler in the midst of the rapprochement crisis, the woman confronted with her mother's death vacillates between longing for the symbiotic mother and terror at being engulfed by her. How she resolves this tension and adapts to the loss is a significant index to her degree of individuation, her own mature sense of self.

Mahler's work, supplemented by the writings of David Gutmann and Otto Kernberg, led me to hypothesize a connection between the failure to separate properly from the mother during the rapprochement subphase and the later adaption to loss that determined the framework for my study. Moreover, Mahler's detailed description of the process in young children serves as the foundation for the scale I developed for assessing separation levels in the study women.

Separation issues are common to any human group—life being at best full of separations that must be dealt with in one way or another—and could be studied as they affect the members of any group. But mother-daughter issues appealed naturally to me, and I especially wanted to see whether a study would reveal motherhood, in and of itself, to be helpful in resolving separation issues left unresolved in earlier life. It seemed logical, on the basis of existing theory, to expect women who have had children to sustain later losses with more ease than women who have not had children. That this did not turn out to be the case was only one of the interesting outcomes of the research project.

Notes

1. Margaret S. Mahler, *The Psychological Birth of the Human Infant* (New York: Basic Books, 1975), 230.
2. Ibid., 228.
3. Ibid., 229.
4. Ibid., 79.
5. Ibid., 227.

3

The Mechanics of a Research Project

W hy do some women fall emotionally ill at the end of their lives while others remain healthy? What makes an older woman feel good about herself and her life? How important are separation issues to these outcomes? Hoping to find answers to these and related questions, my assistants and I set about creating a scientific research project to test the validity of personal and general hypotheses.

We had the goals, the staff, and the still theoretical Separation-Individuation Scale (SIS) whose reliability we hoped to confirm through clinical use. We needed subjects and advertised the need by word of mouth.

Determining the Selection Criteria

The onset of mental illness in older woman has been linked by David Gutmann with failure to separate from the mother, whether or not the mother is still alive.[1] More separated women, in this theory, are expected to adapt better to maternal death than are less separated women, who psychologically "may refuse to let their mother die." The primary research topic under investigation became the importance of separation to later adaptation to loss. The decision to focus on women whose mothers had died followed naturally. This was the first criterion for study subjects.

The second criterion was that all the study women themselves have been mothers. This choice was made on the basis of existing pregnancy literature, which suggests strongly that mothering affords women an additional opportunity to resolve early conflicts. The advantages gained by the mothering experience, insofar as they help restore equilibrium after disruption by the loss of the mother, would have added a potential confound, unless we decided to use more variables than seemed practical (for example, parents versus nonparents). Restricting the subjects to women who were or who had been mothers also made it possible for us to dismiss from consideration the myriad possible causes for childlessness—among which failure to separate would be especially resistant to detection.

Our operational definition of the term *mother* became a woman who had raised at least one child to adulthood. We came to define an older woman as one of sixty or more years of age. Since sixty seems to signify the point of transition into old age, women who have moved past that point provide a perfect testing ground. Issues of separation-individuation are believed to have their greatest impact at this time when the likelihood of sustaining profound losses increases. Additionally, since the problems of menopause have generally been left behind by women in this age group, the potential for distortion of the findings by menopausal effects is reduced.

Other criteria used for the selection of subjects were cognitive endowment (we wanted only women who had high school diplomas or the equivalent because failure to achieve an independent self may be related to a lack of educational opportunity); health (we selected out as ineligible those with known disease processes and women with prior psychiatric histories who had required hospitalization); and financial status (we excluded women at the poverty level since severe financial hardship is a recognized though not universal impediment to the development of autonomy).

With these criteria determined, we sought to increase our awareness that even highly separated women function at less than full capacity during the initial stages of mourning the deaths of their mothers. The elapsed time since the mother's death was therefore used as a grouping factor for investigating two main variables, with the expectation that an interaction effect between them would be revealed. Although originally intended to be five years, the elapsed time criterion was extended one year when it became evident that adaptation to maternal loss is a slower process than had been realized. So women who had experienced the loss of their mothers within the six years immediately prior to the study were assigned to the recently bereaved group, group I, while those women whose mothers had died more than six years earlier were assigned to group II.

At the outset, we predicted that the final analysis would show that

1. The women in the distant loss group would be more separated than the recent loss group
2. The women in the distant loss group would function more adequately than the others
3. The women in the distant loss group would function better only if they actually were more separated than the others

The correspondence between the degree of separation achieved and the recentness of loss was deemed to be of special importance since a hoped-for outcome of this research was information on conditions that promote adaptation. It was possible that the research would show that only those women who had been highly separated at the time of their mother's deaths or had been able to draw on their own mothering or other growth-enhancing experiences were ever able to recover from their losses, while less separated women would never do so.

Finding the Subjects

Through a snowball sampling technique, starting with a few women personally known to me, thirteen women were located to fit the appropriate criteria. The rest of the subjects were found by contacting directors of service organizations as well as senior citizens' centers and adult study groups. No evidence of systematic bias in the sampling methods was revealed in later analysis of the women, using these two sampling procedures.

Maintaining a stable group of subjects proved more difficult than anticipated. Several women who had agreed to take part unexpectedly expressed changes of heart during the course of the study. Even a prospective recruiter reneged on a promise of help because of apprehension about intruding into the lives of recently bereaved women, a concern that frankly I shared before I observed the eagerness of the subjects to share their feelings about their mothers.

Social workers and teachers, on my request, were helpful in recruiting subjects, but most helpful of all were the women who had been chosen to take part. Each of them had names to offer of friends who met the criteria and who were sure to enjoy the experience. And that is how the snowball technique works.

The Chosen Subjects

The subjects who were selected and eventually studied, after some natural attrition, were thirty-nine women who live and work in a large metropolitan area. Some live in areas with high concentration of elderly people, while others live more isolated lives in fashionable suburbs. All are over sixty years of age, all have survived the deaths of their mothers, and all agreed to take part in this study.

The women, all between sixty and ninety years of age, range across levels of educational achievement from a proudly self-educated high school dropout to a doctoral candidate. The number of children averages out to 2.4 for each one. At the time of the study, 66 percent were married, and 19 percent were currently involved in an intimate relationship with a lover or companion. Of the 44 percent who had been widowed and the 10 percent who had been divorced, 10 percent had remarried. Two other interesting statistics: 23 percent had at some time been in individual psychotherapy, however briefly, and 40 percent had combined child raising with a full-time career (except during the period when their children were small).

Additional Features of the Sample and Setting

Most of the women are Jewish (what this very particular characteristic and others mean to the generalizability of the findings to the larger population of women will be discussed).[2] Many reside in the myriad ethnic enclaves that ring the city. As longtime residents, they are inordinately proud of their city's contrasting faces: the booming industry juxtaposed against the beauty of the waterfront, its sophistication and toughness, along with the warmth of its people.

Other unique features of this sample which increase its homogeneity are related to the middle-class origins of the women. For example, one can safely assume that they share similar attitudes toward childbearing, including valuing the child, prolonging the dependency period, and stressing education. Women from such a background would be most likely to at least have some opportunity to develop their cognitive capacities, in contrast to those whose endowments are so limited that survival, much less growth, may be at issue. (The one exception may have been the self-educated mother of thirteen children mentioned earlier, the only black subject in the study.)[3]

The Testing Instruments

The main hypothesis—that women who were separated would function better than women who were not—was investigated along a number of different dimensions, such as work role, interpersonal relationships, and so forth. Functioning was operationally defined by means of a combined overall score based on three separate measures: the Rorschach Psychological Functioning Scale (RPFS); the Harrow Functioning Interview; and the Katz Adjustment Scale (a self-administered symptom checklist). The score obtained from these measures, which are more fully described in the appendix, provides a reliable assessment of the levels of internal and external functioning.

In addition to these tests, the study employed a few cards selected from the Thematic Apperception Test, the TAT cards that provided the basis for developing the new Separation-Individuation Scale (SIS) instrument.

The Study Procedure

Possible participants, selected from among persons known to me, their contacts, and others suggested by the various community resource people I had asked for help, were contacted by telephone and briefed about the proposed research project. If they needed more time to consider their participation, they were sent form letters detailing the goals and procedures involved and asking for their help (see the appendix to this book for a description of these procedures).

If, however, they quickly agreed to take part, they were immediately interviewed over the telephone with respect to the salient facts: When did they lose their mothers? Had they had children? Had they experienced mental illness? The initial screening had fairly well assured affirmative responses to the first two queries—that is, it confirmed that the women had both had children and lost their mothers; it had not, however, provided identification of women with prior psychiatric histories. The question touching on this sensitive but crucially important topic was embedded among several others dealing with general health problems.

As eligible candidates for the research project were selected, they were assigned to one of the groups on the basis of the time elapsed since the deaths of their mothers. Membership in each group closed as predetermined numerical goals were filled. Appointments were made for two separate interview sessions, conducted at the convenience of the subjects and in their own homes.

All the interviews, whether conducted by me or by my assistants, were set up in a semistructured format that allowed various personal themes to be explored as they surfaced. The questions, including those asking for factual information, elicited a great deal of subjective material, all carefully attended to and copiously annotated. At the same time, the complementary use of objective measures that were built into the procedure ensured against researcher bias in the choice of questions. So the SIS and Rorschach tests were administered in varying order according to standard procedures that are recommended for increasing objectivity (administration procedures are discussed in the Appendix). And a modification was made in the administration of the Rorschach test in order to avoid misconstruction of brief responses: respondents were asked to give at least two interpretations of each card so that sparse records would truly reflect genuine inner impoverishment, blocking, or anxiety rather than possible administrative failure on the part of the researcher.

Because the advanced age of the subjects was considered likely to intensify the usual stresses of the testing process, the interviewers made special efforts to establish personal rapport with the women prior to their formal evaluations and to ask their questions in a gentle and nonthreatening fashion. According to plan, we aimed to achieve a cordial but controlled social atmosphere in which the subjects would feel free to express their thoughts fully but without the injection of extraneous elements by the interviewers. It was of overriding importance for us to tap into uncensored thoughts into which primary process thoughts might creep so that the answers would be more true psychologically than carefully deliberated answers tend to be. In the course of switching to secondary process thought, people often tidy their statements in order to "look good" to themselves or to the interviewers. Prompting of any kind was therefore totally forbidden.

The strictures against prompting occasionally proved difficult to enforce, demanding as they did the suppression of the testers' desires to be "helpful" to the subjects in formulating their responses. With careful supervision, these altruistic transgressions were kept to a minimum, and the interviews (each approximately two hours in length) were carried out according to plan.

In the next phase of the study, the test results were scored by eight clinicians thoroughly trained in the use of the chosen instruments. Some results were rated by more than one scorer in order to assess the interscorer reliability (in such instances, the scores were averaged and used for subsequent analysis). The interscorer agreement on the Rorschach Psychological Functioning Scale (RPFS) was 89 percent; the judges disagreed on only two of eighteen occasions. The scorers of the SIS managed to agree 82 percent of the time, which means that the raters arrived at the same diagnostic classification more than four times out of five. All in all, the interscorer reliability for the tests used was quite satisfactory.[4]

The Interviews

The interviews consisted of the following formal components: administration of the Harrow Functioning Interview; the self-administered Katz Adjustment Scale; and two projective tests, administered in alternating order—the Rorschach, and the SIS, the new scale consisting of five TAT cards. In good, tried-and-true interviewing fashion, the women were put at ease by casual conversation, the topics determined by their own interests, before the hard questions—relating primarily to the quality and nature of their interpersonal relationships, especially those with their mothers—were asked.

With subtle shifts, the interviewers introduced the testing measures and asked the questions preplanned to elicit information regarding the following:

the timing, nature, and duration of emotional problems (to create a frame of reference for the emerging symptomatology in relation to the mother's death)

the nature of work relationships (to learn about possible creative or nurturant outlets after the children left home)

the marital relationship (to enable assessment of ways in which individual needs—for support and succor—were met)

the early mother-child relationship, in which the subject is the child (this area was extensively explored to shed light on the original infantile process of separation) the later mother-child relationship, in which the subject mothered her own child(ren)

Each interview culminated with an estimate of separation based on the content and form of the subjects' responses. Certain behaviors carry over from one social situation to another and from childhood to adulthood, so a sensitive interviewer can find important clues to a woman's separation potential in both her verbal and nonverbal communications.

Body language and tone of voice convey as much as her words do about a woman's capacity for warmth and self-acceptance, as well as about her appreciation of the points of view expressed by others. How a woman behaves, how she arranges her own body during an interview may reveal how she relates to others. A good interviewer can *see* whether a subject is aloof and guarded or inappropriately self-disclosing and clinging.

Other aspects of the interview were evaluated from a specific separation perspective. For example, highly verbal, spontaneously productive responses suggest a level of intellectual vitality and capacity that is linked with mature healthy functioning. Good feelings generated in the interview that spill over into the testing session may be a factor here. But since anxiety and the desire to please the interviewer also tend to increase output, the assessment of the quality of a woman's interpersonal relationships rests largely on the substance of her oral statements.

All these factors were taken into consideration when each subject, at the conclusion of the interview, was evaluated by the researcher-interviewer. Overall maturity levels were designated, in separation terms, as (1) unseparated, (2) unseparated to partially separated, (3) partially separated, (4) partially to fully separated, or (5) fully separated. The correlations and conclusions that developed from these assessments will be discussed in detail in chapters 9 and 11.

Notes

1. Loss or threatened maternal loss was often the precipitant to hospitalization in the sample of childless women studied by David Gutmann, suggesting that parenthood may facilitate the working through of separation issues, according to the report in his paper, "The Clinical Psychology of Late Life: Developmental Paradigms" (Presented at the West Virginia Gerontology Conference: Transitions of Aging, Morgantown, W.Va.: May 23–26, 1979).

2. I chose a homogeneous sample, consequently "sacrificing" generalizability for the wished-for significance on the dependent variable of the study (functioning). This choice, as well as the sampling method used, were the result of budgetary considerations.

Although my findings apply only to women resembling the study subjects, one illuminating finding related to the meaning of motherhood transcends socio-economic, cultural, and even generational differences. Specifically, the older women studied varied widely in their ability to use the mothering experience for their own growth, despite the homogeneity of the sample and the fact that all had been mothers. This depended on the kind of mothering they had themselves received, which suggests that no one group has a monopoly on either "good" or "bad" mothering.

Nevertheless, future studies of diverse populations of women—particularly those with different kinds of socializing experiences from ours—may provide useful insights into the meaning of separation for later functioning; for example, the counterparts of the study mothers in cultures in which either the elderly are revered and dependency is fostered in younger persons of both sexes, as in Japan, or women are downtrodden, as in some of the underdeveloped nations of the world.

3. This woman clearly had overcome many obstacles in her life, and indeed her low separation score may be related to early deprivation. However, her performance and the special circumstances of other subjects did not influence the results. For example, between-group comparisons showed no statistically significant differences on any of the variables thought likely to affect separation, such as age, cognitive endowment, educational achievement, health, financial status, involvement in psychotherapy, widowhood, and other losses. See comparisons in Jane B. Abramson, *Evaluation of the Effects of Separation on Adaptation to Loss in Older Women Who Have Lost Their Mothers* (Ann Arbor, Mich.: University Microfilms International, 1985) 48–49.

4. See "Results," in Jane B. Abramson, *Evaluation of the Effects of Separation on Adaptation to Loss in Older Women Who Have Lost Their Mothers* (Ann Arbor, Mich.: University Microfilms International, 1985), 68–84.

4
No One Loves Me—Enough

Psychologically stuck in the rapprochement phase, narcissists are particularly vulnerable to personal losses. They may seem, by all outward signs, to be as competent, as clever, as fascinating as anyone could wish to be. Indeed, the fifteen study subjects who were identified by their variable test scores[1] as highly narcissistic were generally not visibly different from any of the other participants. They exhibited many of the same characteristics as those in the healthiest group, with one vital exception.

Characteristics of Narcissism

Able to function at high levels in response to the normal demands of daily life, the women identified as narcissistic reacted poorly to personal crises. When faced with physical illness or debility, the loss of someone close to them, or any threat to their perceived selves, these women felt shattered. They felt themselves deficient in the inner resources that coping with their situations required. One of the subjects, who had suffered a breakdown when threatened with the imminent loss of her eyesight, showed her continuing fear of losing control over her life by repeated attempts to control the interviewer and the interviewing process; she eventually left the study.

Situations and achievements that serve as positive values in normal lives are of little use to women like this. Personal relationships are generally not gratifying for them. Since intimacy brings back the same threat of symbiotic merger (that is, of losing what separate identities they have managed to achieve) that they experienced toward their mothers in infancy, these women find that relationships feel safer if they are not intimate.

Nor are significant accomplishments that earn private and public acclaim any guarantee of self-esteem. Sometimes the very women with the most impressive records of achievement are the ones to display the deepest feelings of worthlessness and inferiority. Many of them, in their late adult years, are still highly critical of their mothers; almost half the narcissistic women in the study disparaged their mothers, describing them as "unmotherly" or "self-centered."

So there is little surprise in the finding that the narcissistic women have greater difficulty in dealing with the deaths of their mothers. Persistent childhood ambivalence toward their mothers shows up in the correlation between their low separation and adaptation scores. That is to say, they are still fairly "unseparated" and they make less than ideal adaptations to situations that confront them.

Old infantile wishes for nurturing care are often reactivated when narcissistic women become mothers. Motherhood allows them an opportunity to use their babies in pathological though certainly unconscious attempts to fulfill their own unrequited longings for love. Exploitation is likely to take covert forms. Parastic or intrusive mothers are apt to deny their self-abhorrent rejective wishes toward their children by hiding these feelings under layers of excessive and smothering attention. Other self-absorbed mothers may vacillate between showing deep concern for their children and totally neglecting them.

One woman in the study, herself narcissistic, denounced her own mother as "a staunch women's libber who neglected her children," but she was nonetheless unable to provide her own children with optimal mothering when she had the chance. Perhaps no experience teaches better than parenthood does that recognition of a problem is no guarantee of prevention. Even the most deliberate intent to avoid recognized parenting pitfalls often fails to prevent generational recurrence.

That women who suffer early deficits in mothering very often treat their own children as they were themselves treated is exemplified in the following account of Marie, an unseparated and highly narcissistic woman I have been seeing in weekly therapy sessions for approximately one year.

The Case of Marie

Marie is a sixty-year-old woman who came to me because she wanted help in dealing with the escalating demands made on her by her husband, an invalid of many years whose debilitating disease has recently taken a turn for the worse. Despite his illness, he had previously been the "rock" on which Marie's life was founded. Now he not only requires constant care and monitoring of his medications, but he is often incontinent and occasionally exhibits bizarre behavior. Marie becomes inordinately frightened by his uncontrolled weeping, drooling, and hallucinations.

To make matters worse, she is plagued with financial problems. Her only child, a nineteen-year-old daughter, is planning marriage. The costs connected with the upcoming wedding, in conjunction with the mounting medical bills, may force a move from a newly furnished apartment to a less comfortable place. Marie feels that her husband is to blame for the poor financial situation in which she finds herself. He borrowed heavily against his life insurance during what she calls "a demented moment," and now they are in serious debt. Her life-long expectations of financial security in her old age are shattered.

"I may wind up in the poorhouse," she says woefully. While she worries about her future, she also reproaches herself for failing to anticipate her current problems. "Why was I so stupid?" she asks. "Why didn't I see what was coming?"

In further self-criticism, she condemns herself for a recurrent, unforgivably monstrous wish that her husband "one day shut his eyes and die quickly." She sees no other way to lighten the burden under which she is forced to live. Marie weeps easily as she talks about the uncertainties of her day-to-day existence with an invalid. She suffers from global, obsessive anxiety about the future and describes feelings of entrapment, worthlessness, guilt, and envy of others who live without her problems. She complains of vague, generalized pains, periodic sleeplessness, and diminished appetite.

The appetite reduction is a departure from her usual eating habits, habits that brought her weight to 260 pounds. Long given to eating when upset, Marie now finds that eating no longer serves the function it once did; she recently lost 30 pounds with relative ease, "a drop in the bucket," by her own account. For the first time in her life, she is alarmed by her appearance. Since work will soon be necessary rather than the option she formerly exercised at will, she recognizes the need to lose weight. (The bias of employers toward hiring overweight people is well known.) Before this, she was able, despite her grotesquely oversized body, to maintain an illusion of attractiveness, an illusion she was apparently able to project to others since she reports having had numerous lovers in the past.

Meticulously dressed in garments chosen to hide the superfluous flesh, Marie first presented herself to me as a confident, astute, and articulate woman who wanted help with problems in the here and now, problems of coping with a dying husband and a thankless child. She did not mention the fact of her mother's death and generally saw the process of probing her "irrelevant past" as requiring a personal investment with little promise of profit. She readily relinquished this view when she started finding current relevance in reviving childhood memories.

A few sessions revealed the fact that Marie's corpulent body served to hide a vulnerable love-starved child. She had been a fussed-over only child for seven years before being displaced from the center of parental attention by a baby sister (who grew up to enjoy many advantages that Marie felt herself denied). But even before that, she remembers her mother as a self-centered woman who used her little girl to draw attention to herself. Marie was "dressed up, paraded around, and [thereby] made to feel special." She learned to employ exhibitionistic tactics to win parental approval.

Marie now characterizes her mother as a "mother's mother" who fulfilled maternal functions according to traditional cultural expectations, paying scrupulous attention to Marie's physical needs and little if any to her emotional needs. Her mother hovered over her and managed to inhibit her activities whether she was sick or well. She was overprotected throughout childhood and adolescence by her mother's persistent denial of permission for Marie to engage in activities with any perceived potential for risk. Unfortunately, a potential for risk was seen in almost all the activities in which Marie showed interest.

Her recovery periods from a series of childhood illnesses were arbitrarily and artificially prolonged. Her mother kept her home from school and in bed long after the child felt well enough to resume attendance. Marie traces her persistent alarm at falling and her current "nasty, annoying, traveling pains" to the scarlet fever she had at age eleven. "But my mother would not let me walk down the stairs alone much earlier than that," she adds, with only a hint of sarcasm.

Although she and her father had "a mad love affair going before that time," Marie felt totally shunted aside when her sister was born. "I became ugly from that moment on," she reports. Her self-esteem suffered a painful and damaging blow, and she soon began to accept food as a substitute for the love she found unattainable. She ate to excess and by adolescence had an obese body as tangible confirmation of her unlovableness. When she broke her leg during her sophomore year in college, she quit school and checked into a weight reduction spa where she lost 90 pounds. Her father "noticed and was pleased."

Not long after the abrupt end of her college career, Marie met and married an Air Force pilot. Their only child was born, somewhat to their surprise, nineteen years later when Marie was forty years old. This daughter soon became a glaring reminder of Marie's personal deficiencies and vulnerabilities. She left the child care to a nurse and directed her energies toward running the family clothing business.

Now Marie marvels at the cool efficiency she once displayed in the business world. In her highly paradoxical self-image, the competence she had in her early adult years has altogether vanished. She is actually somewhat surprised to find herself still alive at sixty; she had not expected to live longer than her mother, who had died at the age of fifty-two. But aside from what she admits are "inconsequential pains," Marie is in relatively good physical health. Her psychological status is less positive. Some informed speculation about the family constellation may help explain the intrapsychic dynamics that add to Marie's apparent burdens.

Marie as Her Mother's Child

It seems likely—and interpretation such as this must necessarily be inconclusive—that Marie's mother resembled the stereotypical parasitic, intrusive mother that has been the target of invective from the pens of Philip Wylie and Philip Roth, to name just two contemporary writers who have denounced the hovering, smothering, food-lavishing mothers who always know or think they know what is best for their children. From a psychoanalytic perspective, such mothers are believed to harbor unconscious desires to reject their children, either when they are born or when they become threatening. Since such desires seem totally unacceptable on a conscious level, these mothers deny the existence of such feelings even to themselves and go to great lengths to prove, mostly to themselves, what good mothers they are. Denial of the abhorrent becomes a moving force.

The resulting exaggerated parenting almost invariably includes attempts to direct the actions and behavior of the children in ways that best suit the mothers' own rather than the children's needs. (At least one study of obese patients found that the mothers restricted their children's activities out of their own fears of social contacts.[2]) As was suggested earlier, these immature mothers have usually suffered early deficiencies in mothering themselves.

Marie's mother played this overprotective role to perfection. According to Marie, her mother alternated between extremely lavish care and total detachment when Marie's emotional demands seemed excessive, as during adolescence. Discouraged from developing self-reliance and even from achieving appropriate skill mastery, Marie must early have found the world a frightening place. But the secondary gains that came with invalidism—such as increased maternal attentiveness and feeding—led Marie to form conflicting wishes: she wanted both to grow up and to retreat to a safe and familiar milieu. Even now, she invents reasons for staying at home.

Marie's present bewilderment may trace back to her initial reaction to her sister's unanticipated birth (her earliest memory centers on waking up in her sister's unwelcome presence) and to a general absence of consistent maternal support early in life. Immature and realistically unable to fend for herself, she felt herself alone in an unpredictable environment.

Rejection by classmates and neighboring children as she grew up reinforced Marie's determination to become self-sufficient. Food became a source of gratification that she could herself control and regulate, without needing to rely on the emotionally unavailable parents. Her description of a bygone but fondly remembered "mad love affair" with her father suggests a secondary meaning worth noting: Marie may have had wildly erotic fantasies about their relationship and tremendous anger at its termination.

The current paradoxical view of herself as both competent and helpless probably reflects the alternation of paternal acceptance and withdrawal of interest—for which she may hold herself responsible.

ie as Her Child's Mother

Marie does not have an easy time in general developing close relationships with people. Because of early distortions in her love relationships, she experiences people as narcissistic extensions of herself. She hides her dependency, her deep need of people, under an independent, critical facade. She deprecates others to avoid revealing how much she needs them; such an admission would expose her once more to the danger of exploitation and/or abandonment.

Her relationship with her daughter, Alicia, is a constant seesaw affair. She is proud of her daughter but constantly belittles her. She tries to live out unrealized hopes through her daughter's accomplishments and worries whether Alicia will finish her studies, as if her own credentials were at risk—which is to say that she treats her daughter as a narcissistic extension of herself.

Marie's involvement with her daughter was delayed by her own unreadiness to mother. She frankly admits that she would have had an abortion if a legal opportunity had been available when she found herself pregnant. When the baby was born, Marie felt helpless to meet its needs. The baby's vulnerability frightened her. She hired a more competent care-taker and concentrated on her business interests, leaving her former life-style largely intact. The baby was relegated to "a small corner of our life; our existence was too exciting for more." It was only when Alicia reached adolescence and ceased being a living reminder of her mother's helplessness that Marie became deeply involved in her life.

Perhaps it was the convergence of the daughter's growing powers and the husband's enfeeblement that caused Marie to switch her major focus to Alicia. She developed an intense, consuming interest in the girl's activities that was not altogether appreciated by the object of that interest. "Alicia never lets me forget that she did not see her mother for the first five years of her life."

Now that she is threatened with the loss of both her husband and daughter, Marie has come face-to-face with her unacknowledged dependency needs—needs connected to the loss of her own mother as we shall see. "Somehow," she observes sadly, "when you are heavy, everyone expects you to be strong." She has never felt weaker. She has asked for psychiatric help for the first time in her life.

Analysis

Without minimizing the impact of the external circumstances that brought her to crisis at this stage of her life, it is useful to review the key elements that shaped Marie's personality:

1. The overprotective mother discouraged her from moving out and learning new skills; any place but home with mother became a source of terror.

2. She was prevented from becoming self-reliant and autonomous; she was unable to separate appropriately from her mother in childhood.

3. She developed conflicting wishes to grow up and to retreat to a safe, familiar milieu.

4. Her paradoxical view of herself reflects the parents' duality: their early acceptance and later withdrawal of love.

5. The parental rejection damaged her self-esteem at a vulnerable age. While the original trauma occurred early, the continued assaults on the self consolidated the pathology in early adolescence.

6. Her determination to succeed on her own in order to compensate for her father's lost love helped her to function efficiently and to mask the problem through middle adulthood.

Throughout the course of her life, Marie learned to use a number of thought and behavior patterns that help her protect her fragile sense of self. As part of her continued reliance on these defense mechanisms, she now projects the weak, passive aspects of her personality onto her sickly husband. She is terrified when his uncontrolled weeping or bizarre behavior echoes the vulnerability that exists behind her own facade. (She suppresses recognition of that vulnerability—her father would have despised it!)

She actively denies her wish for her husband's death by attending to his every need—just as her mother overdid her nurturing of Marie in order to deny her rejective tendencies—and even sleeps fitfully so that she can make sure that her wish does not come true. She is compulsively, obsessively preoccupied with the imminence of diverse catastrophes. She imagines the most dire outcome of every unresolved situation and then is able to experience relief when her worries turn out to have been exaggerated.

In the most dramatic of her defense mechanisms, Marie has used her obesity to protect herself from the knowledge that slimness will not solve her lifelong problems. It would be painful for her to become aware that no one appreciates her weight loss in the way that her father once did, and moreover, her corpulence serves to hide the depth of her continuing need for the same sort of love and care that she received as a baby.

For no matter how big she becomes in the business world, part of her remains very, very small. Only now when she is faced with the real possibility of multiple losses is she coming to grips with the separation problems that have long bedeviled her. Marie is beginning to see that her failure to go through a proper mourning process after the death of her mother derives from a continuing refusal to "let her mother go" in order to put off true separation.

In a milder variant of the pathology that drives some women to hold regular conversations with their dead mothers in the cemetery (like a patient I once treated), Marie sometimes talks about her mother as if she were still alive, idealizing her in one breath and disparaging her in the next. "My mother was so beautiful that everyone adored her," she reports midway through an account of her own early sense of isolation.

In fact, Marie's futile attempts to wrest undying love from a mother who was beyond her reach even when alive resemble the trials of the toddlers that Mahler observed in her rapprochement study. She saw them as tending "to turn back to mother, to blame her, to demand from her . . . and still to be ambivalently tied to her. They demanded from mother that she settle a debt, so to say."[3] Like those youngsters, Marie keeps an unconscious accounts receivable in which her mother's unremitted obligations to her are recorded. She is stuck developmentally at rapprochement. If she is not always to remain "a little girl," she will have to deal with her painful but long-repressed feelings of anger over her abandonment.

By her recent entry, with psychotherapeutic assistance, into a true mourning process, Marie has taken a vital step toward maturity.

Notes

1. The inconsistent test scores of narcissistic subjects who scored high on overt behavioral measures related to work and social roles and low on internal measures (RPFS) and separation, suggest that a sizable gap may exist between internal living and outward adjustment, according to the "Results," in Jane B. Abramson, *Evaluation of the Effects of Separation on Adaptation to Loss in Older Women Who Have Lost Their Mothers* (Ann Arbor, Mich.: University Microfilms International, 1985), 88.

2. Hilde Brusch, *Eating Disorders* (New York: Basic Books, 1973), 69–70.

3. Margaret S. Mahler, *The Psychological Birth of the Human Infant* (New York: Basic Books, 1975), 106.

5
Pictures Worth
One Thousand Words

Even granting that separation may be a sine qua non for establishing a separate, cohesive self-representation, one may well wonder how it was possible to gauge Marie's failure to achieve separation. First of all, the effectiveness of psychotherapeutic intervention, in disciplines as remote from one another as psychoanalysis and est, hinges on the patient's ability to verbalize innermost needs and cravings. The ability to guide patients to such verbalization is the quintessential art and craft of therapy.

The TAT Cards

For the purposes of my examination of separation-individuation in older women and to guide the subjects to verbalization, I gave Marie and the other subjects picture cards to look at and tell stories about. Selected for convenience from the set of Thematic Apperception Test (TAT) cards that is widely used for research purposes, the cards depict people and situations in a way that permits a broad range of interpretations that reflect the fundamental values of the viewer. Because what is seen and described depends on the individual's enduring view of herself and on her related expectations of others, the narrative descriptions tell more about the viewer than about the object being viewed. Unconsciously, what you see is what you *are*.

The five cards were chosen because they offered pictorial representations capable of stimulating fantasies and emotional responses about mother-daughter relations and were thus relevant to my specific testing objectives. And while for convenience I presented these themes through selected TAT cards, I might just as well have used a virtually limitless variety of other artwork touching on the same themes without expecting a change in the substance of the responses.

For example, a TAT card showing a boy with a violin is able "to elicit feeling and stories dealing with authority" because this picture is "a convenient symbolization of a person in an ambivalent emotional situation."[1] It deals with the general issue of impulse versus control by parental figures. For example, is the boy obliged to practice, or does he rebel and prefer to play outside—two typical plots. Since any number of other pictorial representations are just as capable of plumbing subjective experiences with authority and parental control, I have no doubt that the responses to my Separation-Individuation Scale (SIS), comprised of the TAT subset, were determined by the evocative power of the themes depicted, rather than by the particular delineations used. Accordingly, figures 1 through 5, which differ somewhat from the chosen test cards (but are also labelled SIS cards to avoid confusion), appropriately reflect thematic content.

The story-telling process itself is a deeply satisfying, even therapeutic experience for many women. In contrast to the uncontrollable elements of dreams, their narrative creations about the cards are "safe" fantasies. Their responses must be adapted to the stimulus content of the pictures, which allows them to achieve a measure of control that seems to allay anxiety in some older women. In responding to the cards, unseparated women were for example able to preserve their idealized images of the "good mother" while displacing their own inadmissible anger toward their own mothers onto a witchlike female figure (who was, interestingly, seen as benign by some subjects, reaffirming the significance of thematic content).

The story-telling process seemed to facilitate the working through of separation issues in the study women, but research not therapy was the mutual task. A coding system developed specifically for this study made it possible to categorize the respondents' subjective interpretations of the cards into five levels of separation that are as objective as intrapsychic tools can be.

The major assumption on which the findings rest is that the woman who is still tied to her mother will perceive herself in certain ways that are manifested in the stories she constructs in response to the visual stimuli provided by the thematic picture cards. Since the goal was to have the subjects reveal their unconscious feelings about their mothers, the cards were specifically chosen to elicit fantasy in that specific area. The first three cards were selected for their direct pertinence to that topic, as the representations shown in figures 1, 2, and 3 indicate.

Less obvious choices grew out of the hypothesis that highly separated individuals describe distinct events and people in their stories, regardless of the content of the cards being viewed.[2] In order to provide opportunities to fully separated women to impose their own internal structures on cards devoid of mother-daughter context, I selected the remaining two cards for their ambiguity with respect to mother-daughter (and other interpersonal) relations. These are represented by figures 4 and 5. Not surprisingly, of all

Figure 1. SIS Card Number 1

the five cards presented to the participants in the study, card 1 was the most revealing with respect to separation issues.

The study women were instructed merely to look at the cards (one at a time) and to narrate the events pictured. They were told that there are no clues other than the picture, no right or wrong answers to worry about and that they should simply tell the story in as much detail as seemed right to them. One story can be very revealing: tests of internal consistency showed a high degree of cohesiveness in the SIS stories told by any one subject so that performance on one item serves as a reliable predictor of the total outcome.[3]

Before examining the creations of some of these women, I hope that readers will submit to this simple process themselves. I suggest that they take a good look at figure 1 and write down the story it seems to tell them. This invitation to self-analysis is a way of moving through the work with heightened insight and self-understanding. It is a very effective method of personalizing the subject matter, enabling us to share in the insights of the author, because we wear the same shoes, so to speak.

For example, some of the women's stories are filled with anger and hostility, or have embedded in them resistance to looking further. We can see this in our own reluctance to test the waters. Moreover, we can participate with them in their pain and suffering as well as their exultation by finding resonant chords in our own experience. And we can differentiate between them and ourselves by seeing where we fit in.

For it is only through understanding ourselves that we can hope to understand other people—which the wisest people in psychology know so well. That is why as part of their training they may test themselves first (and ideally, undergo a personal psychoanalysis) before subjecting others to the same experience. But even if the SIS is not used in this way (as a teaching tool), we have profited immeasurably as a result of simply using the exercise for enrichment. Self-examination is inherently rewarding.

Subject Responses

Let us next examine the stories created by three narcissistic women (supplementary evidence confirmed the indications of narcissism in their test scores). Note the similarity of emotional tone in these productions and the consistently negative feelings toward the mother that are expressed in the italicized phrases.

The first subject, Marie, took a long look at a picture along the same thematic lines as figure 1 and described the interaction between the woman and the little girl (in the original TAT card used in the study, the child who

Figure 2. SIS Card Number 2

was seated close beside the woman seemed to be avoiding eye contact) this way:

> This is a mother giving advice to her daughter—and *she is not terribly interested.* She is reading something that has a moral or something she wants her daughter to understand and believe in. And the daughter is looking off into space, *wanting much more to be outside playing* or playing with her doll than listening to her mother philosophize.

[Question: What is the daughter feeling?]
Resentment at being held there. She wants to be some place else rather than where she is.

With the same card in hand, Rachel says:

[I see] a girl with a doll in her lap, and her mother gives her some advice, but as kids usually do, *she doesn't listen.* The daughter is *much prettier than her mother* and already has plans of her own. She feels that *what is good enough for her mother is not good enough for her.* She has big plans with herself, and being a mother herself does not play an important role. Her mother knows she has high-flying dreams.

Later on, when the girl is grown up—thanks to her practical and earthy mother—she is spared the worst and finally marries a man just like her father and . . . is no better off.

Jeannette expresses difficulty in recognizing the objects represented but still has a lot to say:

Doll or baby? Doll. Can't make this out. A book? *No rapport between mother and daughter; mother more interested in what the book will tell her than what her daughter will tell her. The daughter is upset; mother is oblivious.*

The daughter cannot wait to grow up and be a mother—be better than her mother—she loves that doll, though she is not holding it like you would expect her to. She looks upset; usually girls handle babies like that when they are upset. She *must be upset with mother and is taking it out on the doll. Real problem building up in the family.*

All the above stories reflect a pseudoindependent, *au contraire* attitude typical of narcissistic women; they tend to reveal their negative feelings toward mother/mothering by ignoring or downplaying the maternal representation in the picture, by articulating a child's rejection of the mother's intentions or advice, and by projecting a wish to be elsewhere, to be acting independently. Compare the mother-daughter relationships described in these stories with the ones in the three that follow. The feelings toward mother, once again italicized, are now positive rather than negative.

Figure 3. SIS Card Number 3

Card 1 prompts Audrey to fantasize thus:

The mother says, "Let's have a moment together, I want to read you something." The little girl says, "Yes." It turns out the way it always does; the mother finishes reading, and the little girl goes off to play. It's a *card of a mother and daughter spending time together.*
[Question: What feelings are involved?]
Usually those are very sweet moments between mother and daughter, very warm between them. A lovely moment.

Mona interprets the same scene:

It looks like a mother and daughter with a good relationship between them: the way the mother reads to her child, spends time with her child. The way the child is holding the little doll in her hand; she's just holding it, it isn't being threatened in any way. The mother is reading to the child, cementing the relationship.
From the way the girl looks, *it's an ongoing thing, something they do on a daily basis, a nice family relationship.* It turns out very well. As the child grows and matures, *she will always remember this closeness with her mother.* Both look calm.

And, in the last example, Rosalie gives this brief description:

It's a darling picture. Mother is a little sad that her little girl is growing up. *The sofa seems to be enveloping them, serving as a kind of a nest, a refuge.*

Participating readers might ask themselves which type of story their own most resembles.
What does it say about them? How would one judge?

Evaluation of Subject Responses

Since psychologists draw meaningful generalizations about the personalities of the speakers not only from what individuals say but also from the way they express themselves, form as well as content is generally taken into consideration during the evaluation process. Such form variables as story length, word usage, organization, type and extent of imagery, and indications of nervousness or self-censorship all give important clues about the

Figure 4. SIS Card Number 4

storyteller. A very brief plot may indicate emotional constriction. The provision of alternative outcomes suggests indecisiveness and ambivalence.

Greatest attention naturally is focused on the narrative's content: the description of characters portrayed, the setting visualized for them, and the interactions between them. Of all the content variables, the basic plot (or theme) is of crucial importance. It is analyzed for dynamic structure and for what it reveals about the person's feelings, values, and expectations. And if the content of one fantasy creation tells a lot about a person, looking at the pattern of responses in a series of stories uncovers more. With that option, the interpreter looks at the content from a number of angles: Are men and women habitually seen in set ways? Are women always passive, men always dominant? Are story resolutions consistently happy or sad? Are important figures in the pictures omitted from the stories? Special attention is given to themes that seem to recur in a subject's narratives—hopefulness, isolation, pessimism, ambivalence—since such repetitions suggest the existence of a special thematic screen through which the subject views and interprets reality. In fact, such thematic repetitions suggest strong affective predispositions on the part of the storyteller, whose own deeply embedded tensions lie beneath plots involving conflicts between desires, frustrated impulses, unmet needs, and yearnings for magical outcomes.[4]

To illustrate the use of these analytic techniques, let us return to Marie's description of card 1. Note how she expresses the child's anger and "resentment at being held there." This description reveals the defenses against emerging love that have been developed by a woman for whom loving others means ceasing to exist as "a person in one's own right." Such resistance to love is an obstacle to separation since the completion of the separation process depends on the reanimation of loving feelings toward the mother.

But the very fact that the girl (standing in for Marie) remains in the picture is a hopeful sign, showing a longing to regain, simply by being there, some measure of love from the mother. The implication that there has been something of value in the past relationship shows conflicting rather than overwhelmingly negative feelings about mothering. Such conflicting feelings are considered signs of a higher level of separation than are indicated by total rejection.

Though one interpretation of one story may help us understand one woman's level of separation, it is only in combination with information derived from other such interpretations that it can lead to meaningful conclusions for research or practical purposes. So before we go any further with the interpretations of the responses to the thematic picture cards, readers will need to know something about the system used to assess those responses. This system is a new one, created out of necessity, for although

Figure 5. SIS Card Number 5

the indexes of separation to which I refer are well established in the theoretical literature, there has long been a need for a practical tool to be used in measuring separation levels in a standardized fashion.

The Separation-Individuation Scale

The Separation-Individuation Scale (SIS) that I developed in order to quantify the levels of separation achieved by the women in this study has an intrinsic potential for wider application. It has already proved itself to be a valid and reliable instrument. When it has been appropriately cross-validated on other test populations, I am confident that its use will give psychologists a vitally important perspective on adult female development. Since the early childhood separation process is in many ways analogous to a woman's adult development—as aspects of her identity are again subjected to the emotional pulls and tugs of a mother-child context—separation theory, and this index of separation, may provide a way to measure maturity in any stage of life by gauging a woman's relationship with her mother as she moves from a primitive attachment to a more and more differentiated state.

The SIS measure can, for example, be useful in charting a woman's progress in terms of her attachment to her mother as her attachment to her own child (or children) wanes and waxes. The expectation is that test findings will reveal, over a period of years, whether the woman's residual dependency issues are reactivated—and/or resolved—as she passes important milestones in her mothering career. The scale may permit greater insights into other components of the mothering process as well, but should in any case facilitate professional understanding of separation issues.

The conceptual aspects of the SIS measure are simple enough. Its five levels cover the spectrum of separation-individuation from I to V, with level V representing the balanced and optimally separated self. Psychotics, not present in the sample, would be at level I, borderline psychotics at level II, narcissistic personalities at level III, and psychoneurotics at level IV. Because complete separation is possible in theory only, the fifth level is viewed as an open-ended phase.

The responses to the SIS cards are categorized according to criteria that reflect the underlying dimensions of separation-individuation: balance, integration within the self, acceptance of dependency, and interrelatedness with other people. The following description of typical behaviors shows the progression from level to level that provides the rationale for the categorization.

Level I: The Infantile Self. The woman whose sense of self is so enfeebled that she cannot function unassisted in the outside world is unlikely to be found among the subjects of such a study or among the readers of this book. To such a person, the world may seem to be falling apart, reflecting her own tumultuous inner state. Fantasies evoked by pictured characters are beyond her scope; responses to the SIS cards are marked by unrelatedness.

Level II: The Fluid Self. At this level, there is a real danger of protracted fragmentation of the self because of a seriously defective self-structure. The woman with a fluid self is apt to behave as follows:

1. She may exhibit loose ego boundaries by forgetting that she is telling a story or by going off on tangential subjects. In less severe cases (levels

II–III), she may see women as interchangeable or may describe the protagonist of the story in vague terms (level III).

2. She may resort to a primitive form of idealization, an ego defense that lets her share in the greatness of the highly idealized object in the story as a protection against aggression, or she may so overidentify with one of the characters that the story she weaves becomes a story she is experiencing. This "projective identification," in which the subject almost gets inside the character she is describing, suggests a need to attack and control before she herself is attacked and destroyed.

It is not uncommon for the woman with a fluid self to seem to become her own mother in her story, perhaps to exercise control over her mother from within.

3. She may profoundly reject mothering, so intensely does she fear becoming her own "bad mother." Because the boundaries between her self and others are so fluid, she may barely know herself from the mother who dominates her existence.

4. She may engage in demanding, clingy relationships, or alternatively remove herself from other people. There is no real dependency in the sense of love for those close to her; those others are inevitably dropped from conscious awareness when they cease providing gratification.

Women at this level reveal themselves by departing from common plots related to the pictures (these common plots are summarized in table 5–1). They are likely to see the characters in their stories as capriciously dropping or replacing one another and to see estrangement in scenes that do not reveal it to others.

Level III: The Fragile Self. The partially separated woman whose sense of self is tenuous may behave in the following ways:

1. She may experience others as either narcissistic extensions of the self, or amorphous presences, as others do not exist for such a person. She will mention the persons on card 2 without differentiating between them; her story will not exceed the limits of the card.

2. She may tend to use such psychological defense mechanisms as splitting, whereby the ego splits the self or the experienced self of a significant other person into "good" and "bad" elements and internalizes the parts as separate, unrelated characters; and idealization so that the older woman in card 3 becomes idealized as a kindly crone, an older friend, or a good mother; or, in diametric opposition, is devalued into a witch, a gossip, or a bad mother (older females are often described as bossy or intrusive, even by older females).

3. She may indicate rejection of the nurturing role in her description of card 1 (this card gives important clues to covert maternal relations and is used exclusively to illustrate this dimension). She may talk of the child's

Table 5-1
Common Plots in Response to TAT Cards[a]
(Given by Subject Women)

Card 1: an older woman sitting beside a little girl with a doll

1. A mother performing a motherly function with her child—teaching, advising, or consoling
2. A woman and a child reading for pleasure or entertainment

Card 2: a scene in the country populated by three figures: a man working in the fields, a
woman looking on, and a younger woman holding a book

1. A young girl leaves the farm either for
   a) further education, or
   b) for opportunities not available at the farm
2. People have a tough life gaining a living from tilling the soil

---

Card 3: a close-up view of two female figures: a young woman and an older one, differentially
perceived as benign or malignant.

1. The older woman, who bears a family relationship to the younger woman, is seen as influencing or advising her in some way
2. In one third of the stories, a second plot appears in which the older woman is a symbolic representation of the younger woman

---

Card 4: A young woman's head against a man's shoulder

1. Two love partners are in close embrace in an ambiance of contentment and nurturance
2. Two partners embrace because one is leaving
3. Two partners embrace after a separation

Card 5: A rowboat on the bank of a stream

1. Sheer fun and adventure stories abound, all centering on people who have left their boat for reasons related to their adventure

---

[a]This chart incorporates the summaries of responses to TAT cards first reported by William E. Henry in *The Analysis of Fantasy: The Thematic Apperception Technique in the Study of Personality* (New York: Robert E. Krieger, 1973).

being forced to care for the doll/baby or may ignore the mother or the child. (Perceiving the doll/baby as a representation of an inanimate object such as a vegetable suggests a more primitive level [II] than this one.)

Conflicting dependency wishes and fears suggesting a desire to be both autonomous and a baby (levels III-IV) may contrast here with an unambivalent rejection of mothering (level III). Some will see the girl as simultaneously caring for the doll and yearning to venture out into the world, a view that reflects the viewer's symbolic clinging to mother while she rejects her (level III-IV).

A level III aversion to motherhood is indicated in Marie's description of the scene in card 1, wherein the daughter is "looking off into space, wanting to be outside playing, rather than listening to her mother philosophizing." Rejection of motherhood rates a lower value on the scale than does ambivalence, which is seen as a step toward rekindling loving feelings toward the mother that are prerequisite for the completion of separation.

4. She may also indicate problems in dealing with other people by creating distance between herself and others or by establishing very superficial relations. Some women reveal this distancing trait by seeing the pictured characters as historical or literary figures, while others reduce the entire task of story telling to an intellectual exercise, transforming the problems into intergenerational conflicts of an impersonal nature without reference to any emotional experiences whatsoever. (Paradoxically, some level III women—relying on a reverse distancing mechanism—cling tenaciously to other people. Clinging behavior is an expression of the other side of the conflict—the wish for closeness beneath the distancing behavior.

In sum, responses at this level are characterized by the use of defenses such as splitting and distancing and by an inability to integrate thoughts and feelings. Another particularly significant trait is the experience of other people as part of the self: an inability to recognize ego boundaries, as in the case of parents who intensely live out their own aspirations through their children.

Such a distorted view of one's self and the world inevitably affects interpersonal relationships. The tendency to deprecate others stems from an unwillingness to admit needing them and thereby exposing the vulnerable self anew to the childhood danger of exploitation. Being close to others carries the risk of annihilation through engulfment. Still, the very closeness that is avoided out of fear is just what the incomplete self craves. There is no way to fill the void in women beset with such conflicting strivings, although it is possible for many of them to function well on a superficial level if they have strong support systems on which to rely.

Level IV: Between Partially and Fully Separated. Some measure of overlap between levels is expected. This level is used for responses that fall midway between levels III and V.

Level V: The Balanced Self. The optimally separated woman sees herself as distinct and totally separate from others and is therefore likely to behave in the following ways:

1. She will describe precise events and persons in her fantasies, clearly delineating the characters and relating a story that does not exceed the parameters of the visual representation.

2. She will integrate various aspects of the self into one whole self-representation so that there is no fragmentation and all the diverse elements are meaningfully organized. A story that takes all the myriad details on card 2 into account would qualify as being at level V; a tendency to be obsessed with detail (carrying a good thing to extremes) would, however, suggest a drop on the scale to level IV.

3. She will indicate acceptance of the nurturing role since completion of separation in adulthood presumably depends upon an enhanced ability to love via the mother-child relationship.[5] This is shown by responses to card 4, that describe reconciliation with a mother figure (or the maternal in the man, due to the sexually ambiguous nature of this card); to card 2 that speak of return to the home; to card 1 that describe paying attention to or heeding the advice of mother; and by seeing the older female figure in card 3 as nurturant.

4. She will view people as interrelated, since it is inconceivable for someone to be both whole and separate except in relation to other human beings. Characters may be seen as offering support, advice, succor, or any other positive interaction that affirms the connectedness between the represented figures.

The responses at this level clearly reflect a sense of balance. The more separated woman holds an objective view of herself and the world that may be manifested in her interpersonal relationships—her capacity for intimacy, for example, or her ability to take on the viewpoint of someone else.

The Scoring Process

These summaries of the full range of scoring levels that may be determined from the story-telling exercise bring us directly to the scoring process itself. Categorization of the individual stories relies on another 1 through 5 scoring system that exhibits the range of separateness, from minimum to maximum, exhibited in the teller's tale. The standards for measuring the dimensions of separation were set by the stories told by separated women.

The separated women were identified by the stories that they told, and the intrinsic difficulty of recognizing the standardsetters during the standardsetting process was overcome in small increments. As in the case of the primacy-of-the-chicken-or-the-egg conundrum, one simply must start somewhere and keep refining. Just as creating the first chicken-and-egg logically required simultaneous and interrelated design, the development of the scale required prior conceptualization of the dimensions of separation and of the potential responses that separated individuals would be likely to make, all of these more or less calculated guesses based on theory and psychodynamic understanding.

The tentative expectations for responses reflecting the different levels of separation had to be sharpened and redefined as the actual responses to the visual stimuli were gathered. Protocols that best exemplified the various levels were set up as scoring guides; all the responses given by the subjects were both scored according to the separation yardstick and used to validate or modify its applicability. Eventually it became possible to identify the most separated subjects because their actual stories fell into the highest hypothetical level.

Extrapolating from the form and substance of the fantasy creations of the most separated subjects, I was able to isolate firm dimensions of separation. Analysis revealed that certain features were typical of the stories told by separated women: the heroines consistently perceived others as distinct and separate persons—as mirror images of the narrator's self, the story characters appear to be differentiated and affectively alive, rather than undifferentiated and bland. Therefore, *dimension number one is distinctness.*

The heroines see others realistically, because good and bad are integrated within the self (mother is therefore neither overvalued nor depreciated). Therefore, *dimension number two is integration within the self.*

The heroines of the stories give and receive love freely and take the mother's advice because dependency needs are acknowledged (one can lose oneself in another without losing or diminishing one's self). Therefore, *dimension number three is acceptance of dependency.*

The stories' heroines perceive the world as nurturing and giving, which corresponds with the storytellers' own innate sense of goodness (valuing the self permits the appropriate valuation of others). Therefore, *dimension number four is interrelatedness.*

These carefully distilled criteria provide the reference points for the analysis phase, when each story conjured up in response to seeing the cards is dissected and evaluated for its separation content—that is, for its evidence of distinctness, integration within the self, acceptance of dependency, and interrelatedness—and then is given a point score for each of these dimensions of separation. For one example, table 5-2 illustrates the way that Dimension number one is scored.

Using similar scoring for the other dimensions, a perfectly well-integrated, lucid story in which dependency is accepted as part of a positive interpersonal relationship qualifies for the maximum total of twenty points is shown in table 5-3.

The scoring possibilities for stories devised with respect to card 1 are set forth in table 5-4.

Now, really to understand the scoring process, take another look at Marie's story about card 1, which revolves around the two protagonists from essentially different worlds. The girl tunes out her mother, who "is reading something that has a moral or something that she wants her daughter to understand or believe in. And the daughter is looking off into space, wanting much more to be outside playing."

Closely analyzed according to the scale criteria, the story earned thirteen points on the basis of the factors shown in table 5-5.

Table 5-2
Scoring of Dimension Number One: Distinctness

Degree of Dimension	Points
Describes events precisely	5
Describes events less precisely	4
Midway between 1 and 5	3
Describes events vaguely	2
Fails to describe events	1

Table 5-3
Illustration of a Perfect Score

Story Traits	Points
Describes distinct events	5
Integrates elements into cohesive account	5
Characters accept nurturance	5
Characters relate interpersonally	5

Saved by the bonus point from being a classic level III response, the story is, nonetheless, a typical narcissistic production. It features a mother who is experienced as omnipotent as well as intrusive; the daughter ignores her in an effort to ward off any intrusion (to do otherwise might mean an admission of neediness that is threatening). The story expresses anger at the mother and ambivalence about leaving her which is very close to its surface and has a layer of dependency just below. A description of a personality divided against itself is neatly encapsulated in this story, which pegs the teller, tentatively, at level III; the formidable body of supporting information available to us about Marie confirms the validity of the categorization.

Though the interpretation of one story, standing on its own, can only produce a tentative assessment, its contribution is considerable when it is added to the larger pool of information available to the interpreters working on a research project. When used for diagnostic purposes in therapy, the analysis of a single story would prompt the therapist to amass more information, to search for corroboration, and to dig for deeper meanings. My enthusiasm for the SIS measure should not convey the impression that reliance on it can create a differential diagnosis. It can, however, be a helpful factor in carefully building up the body of evidence required for that purpose.

Evaluating the Scores

At this point participating readers may wish to know what their creative descriptions of the situation depicted in card 1 reveal about them. A few

Table 5–4
Rating of Functioning

Point Score	Level	Rating
17–20	V	Very good
13–16	IV	Good
9–12	III	Fair
6–8	II	Poor
0–5	I	Unable to function outside hospital

Table 5–5
Scoring of Marie's Story to Card 1

Factors that Fulfill Level III Criteria	Points
1. Figures are described as extensions of self	3
2. Use of defenses	3
3. Rejection of nurturing	3
4. Indication of interpersonal problems	3
Plus:	
For expression of conflict over mothering, a bonus point	1
TOTAL	13

words of caution: any similarity between one's story and Marie's creation needs to be understood better. A single narcissistic performance does not mark one as a pathological narcissist, and furthermore a measure of narcissism has redeeming qualities. Its actual life-enhancing value is proved by a moment's reflection on the attention that must be paid to bodily needs and physical appearance in the interest of good health and well-being.

The conventional wisdom that holds a little neurosis to be healthy and some neurotic behavior to be normal derives from the recognition that all our personalities have narcissistic and neurotic features side by side with so-called normal ones. A complex mix of diverse psychological components determines where, at any given moment, we belong on the continuum of psychological functioning that has conceptual space for the mentally deranged, the paragons of mental health, and the rest of us.

Although diagnostic labeling and categorization serve useful purposes in clinical work, the self-testing opportunities in these pages are meant to provide readers with a few insights into the processes used in professional settings, not to condemn them to psychological perdition. Therefore, the fantasies they have spun about card 1 should be analyzed gently and the scores taken lightly and with a grain of salt.

Readers should score their stories according to the dimensions of separation detailed earlier, allocating up to five points each for the degree of distinctness of character delineation, the degree of integration of the component parts into a cohesive account, the acceptance of nurturance by and the interrelatedness by the characters. So a lucid, well-integrated story in which the characters have warm and loving relationships qualifies for a perfect score of 20.

One's score could fall short of perfection by three points and still indicate the level of psychic separation demonstrated by the most highly separated women in the research project. In fact, the study women scored an average of 56 points for the five cards—a narcissistic average of 11.2 points for each story.

While the scoring process succeeds in quantifying, for comparative purposes, some common and less than common elements of the fantasies spun by women in response to the stimuli provided by the SIS cards, the analysis leaves, in each instance, an untapped reservoir of information about the creator of the stories.

Let us see what we can learn by drawing from these unplumbed depths.

Notes

1. William E. Henry, *The Analysis of Fantasy: The Thematic Apperception Technique in the Study of Personality* (New York: Robert E. Krieger, 1973), 48.
2. See discussion of central figure, ibid., 77–78.
3. See SIS results, in Jane B. Abramson, *Evaluation of the Effects of Separation on Adaptation to Loss in Older Women Who Have Lost Their Mothers* (Ann Arbor, Mich.: University Microfilms International, 1985), 77.
4. William E. Henry, *The Analysis of Fantasy: The Thematic Apperception Technique in the Study of Personality* (New York: Robert E. Krieger, 1973), 83.
5. Therese Benedek, "Parenthood as a Developmental Phase: A Contribution to the Libido Theory," *Journal of the American Psychoanalytic Association* 7(1959):389–417.

6
Another Picture to Ponder

I f readers are willing to probe into the secrets of their unconscious processes a little more, they might study card 3 (figure 3) and then compare their fantasy with the stories stimulated in other women by a thematically similar card. Then notice how overwhelmingly negative the following group of stories is, how powerless the protagonist of each one is portrayed as feeling. (The italics underscore negative feelings toward maternal figures.)

Subject Responses to SIS Card 3

Negative Responses

Alice, who mistakenly imagined herself to be expressing universal perceptions, said this:[1]

> *Who is this bitch in the background?! Woman in background is portrayed with such a great deal of meanness, hardness, evil; surprised it's made so plain and vivid in the portrayal—could be done without so much luridness* even though she's not looking at the young woman. She's there as an instrument of meanness. *I assume bitchiness is directed toward the young woman* and also toward others. Older woman will spread gossip, untruths, break up whatever good relationship the young woman has. If the older woman stays in the same environment as the younger woman, *she will make her life miserable. The younger woman doesn't look strong enough to defend herself.*

Sonya builds a tale of intrigue inspired by the Du Maurier novel, *Rebecca*. The evil housekeeper in her story embodies the "bad" part of herself that threatens to destroy the good that is in her. The malevolent mother is within:

> Well, this reminds me of *Rebecca*. This woman is beautiful and *the woman behind her is evil. This man lost a wife who was beautiful. Their housekeeper wants to destroy the second wife.* It turned out well—the second wife was an evil person herself. The evil woman was defeated.

In a perceptive variation on the same theme, Rachel cuts her mother down to size by representing her as a shadowy background figure:

> *Apparently [the picture is of] a young woman and an ugly old woman behind her. If you look closely, there is a similarity,* even though one is pretty and the other ugly. . . . *I would prefer to call [the old woman] a shadow,* which is what Henry James, no, William James called it. *It might be what she will be when she is old, but it also acts in the present, of what we all might be afraid of.*

For Marie, who also perceives the older and younger woman as aspects of a divided self, the mother is not nearly as frightening:

> It could very well be that *this young lady is picturing herself as an old hag,* an old crone. This is what she sees herself becoming. Or *this is what her evil thoughts are like—old and withered and ugly, because the old crone is ugly.* I don't think the lady likes herself very much. Very prissy, very formal, very worried about what the world thinks about her.

The first story is filled to overflowing with bitterness. The venomous feelings of the creator spill over into her fantasy. To an observer trained in psychoanalysis, references to "a bitch" and "bitchiness" provide such overwhelming evidence of hostility on the part of the speaker toward her mother that reconciliation would not be considered a likely development.

The stories that follow reveal the more ambivalent responses of narcissistic women who want to hold on to mothers toward whom they feel very hostile. They manage this by adroit use of "splitting."

In this respect, as in others, the narcissistic woman operates like the rapprochement child. Such a child, whose "good and bad me" are as yet unintegrated, might wonder: "If mommy is all good, how can she abandon me, even when I am bad? But why should I care? I don't need her anyway." The narcissistic woman thinks along parallel lines: "If my good self is all good, how can it abandon me even when my bad self acts out or gets angry? Who needs it anyway?"

While such contradictory feelings can and do exist side by side in the very young child or in the narcissistic woman, the normal adult attempts to erase the contradictions. A "logical" explanation or a switch from primary to secondary process thought may resolve the conflict in favor of integration. But this is not to suggest that a response to card 3 that "splits" the characters into "good" and "bad" is a sign of abnormality, especially since there seems to be a solid likelihood that the configuration and appearance of the figures on this card are particularly conducive to producing responses that involve splitting.

Positive Responses

The idea that the older figure can be seen as a benign or nurturing character is validated by the stories that follow. They are the integrated, balanced responses of three women who inhabit a world refreshingly different from the limited world of the narcissists. The positive expectations and feelings attributed to their characters (indicated by italics) arise from their own harmonious centers.

Katherine manifests pleasure in reminiscing as she tells her tale (reminiscing may well serve an integrative function in old age):

[I see] a picture of a young woman and an older woman. The older woman seems to have the expression that *she's vicariously enjoying the youth of the younger woman. She doesn't have an envious look, though,* but seems to be enjoying it.

Asked how the story turns out, she continues:

Just life; nothing serious is going to happen. *Doesn't seem to have real evil or bad look on her face—neither of them do.*

Isabel also found something good in her mother to reflect in the story:

This could be a story about innocent youth—the old lady saying, "Wait until she knows what I know." Yet the old lady is not unhappy. She is thinking, I had a good time, while it lasted. The old lady is wise.

Nanette finds continuity within her own life cycle, relating the scene to her own experience as a grandmother. She sums up her life like this:

This may be a *grandmother with her granddaughter.* She may be explaining the hardships she has gone through in her life. This woman has lived her life, and the young woman is going to live her life and is looking towards the future. *It turns out very well. The young woman would be listening to the old woman, her grand-mother; she would have gained from the experience."*

The preceding stories, which are perfectly balanced and wholly inte-grated fantasy creations for older women (for whom reminiscing is an enriching experience), contrast markedly with the idealized interpretation of reality expressed by Estelle. Note the merger of mother/daughter into one and the imaginary twinship as she speaks:

Gee—this is a picture of a pretty young woman. The older woman might be her mother, and they look like they might be modeling for this picture. The young one is wondering if she will be a successful model and the old one looks like she's just going along with the young one. It is a nice thing to do, to model, and *some-thing nice may come out of it—money or maybe a marriage proposal—for the young one, I mean.* What happens next is that *they'll be successful models* and the young one will have a very happy marriage, both financially and otherwise.

Scoring Responses

In evaluating their own responses to card 3, readers may compare them with these creations. A perfect score of 15 points may be assigned if the story has distinct characters, is integrated into an inclusive whole, and describes the older woman as motherly or benign. Because interrelatedness, the fourth dimension of separation, is not tapped by this depiction, the perfect score in this instance is obtained by gaining 5 points for each of the other three. From that ideal score, one point is deducted for each of these compo-nents: a view of the older figure as a symbolic representation; a description of the older figure as ugly, loathsome, or oppressive; a plot involving a hostile interpersonal relationship, or other portents of gloom and doom.[2]

For this card, a score of 13–15 points rates as very good, 10–12 as good, 8–9 as fair, and 6–7 as poor. A perfect score on this card identifies a woman who is so secure about her own identity that she does not allow the world to dictate how she feels about her own aging (and she therefore overrides the perceptual tendency to split).

Further Analysis

But this simple scoring system should not obscure the wealth of infor-mation that all the stories, including the reader's, can reveal about their creators, as the following analysis illustrates. For the purpose of looking below the overt or manifest meaning to the covert or latent meaning, let us return to Sonya's response to card 3:

> Well, this reminds me of *Rebecca*. This woman is beautiful and the woman behind her is evil. This man lost a wife who was beautiful. Their housekeeper wants to destroy the second wife. It turned out well—the second wife was an evil person herself. The evil woman was defeated.

In-depth analysis suggests a new theme: father as well as mother plays an important role in female development from early on. Primary process thought is a category wherein contradictory feelings can peacefully coexist in mental life, and it is a category, therefore, filled with the irrational thoughts of young children, the utterings of schizophrenics, and the dreams of almost everyone. As an example of primary process thought, this story has many levels beneath its surface.

On one level, the story poses the threat that a part of this woman can destroy another part. On another, the crime of matricide is played out—in the death of the second wife—in a scenario that shrouds the characters in secrecy so that the perpetrator of the crime can escape responsibility for the imagined deed (such ambiguity keeps dreamers from awakening and keeps Sonya from lapsing into a stony silence). On still another level, there is the wish-fulfilling oedipal victory of the child within her. While Freudians would be predisposed to take this view, I lean toward an interpretation that provides for the overlap of oedipal and separation issues.

From Sonya's first words ("This reminds me . . .") we learn that this is an "old story," originating in childhood. The convoluted plot then unfolds. Father is introduced ("this man") and Mother is killed off ("the evil woman is defeated") but not without justification ("the second wife was a bad person herself"). The father is thus left with "the house-keeper," who fills a variety of roles. She embodies both the little girl's badness (her forbidden wish to take Mother's place with Father) and the resurrected beauty who woos Father away and whose dirty work she carries out. The housekeeper and Rebecca live on in the picture as dual aspects of the woman because the child had done no more than wish the mother dead.

So it "turns out well" (nothing happened), which is what can happen when the storyteller, or dreamer, writes the script and plays all the parts as well. In unconscious scripts, the usual rules of syntax do not apply. Players switch roles like characters in a Pirandello play, but the storyteller always survives since it is her essence that gives life to every character. One character epitomizes the teller more than the rest; in this case, it is the evil house-keeper/beautiful Rebecca.

Like many a drama performed on the stage, this one cannot to be taken at face value. In its dynamic meaning, the child in the woman is saying that Father disappointed her when he gave up the love of his life, his little girl. The fact that he is the one who suffers (his first wife dies) makes the pain more bearable. Because Mother will not abandon her as long as she denies the true meaning of her story (in the same way young children deny their own truths when they imagine Mother to have guessed their innermost secrets), Sonya has created a story that allows fulfillment of altogether contradictory wishes. She eats her cake and saves it for another day.

Sonya's fantasy, like many fairy tales with thinly disguised oedipal themes, allows good to triumph over evil, making it safe for her to pretend without actually destroying those she loves. Relying on a defense against anxiety and guilt known as "undoing," she lets the mother she has wanted to defeat but cannot afford to lose survive in the "good me." Or perhaps the entire story is an attempt to even the score magically, to "redo" a period in her life when she felt powerless before apparently omnipotent adults.

Regardless of the actual facts of her childhood, the facts related in her story are emotionally true for Sonya. The fact that her fantasy replicates the plot of a novel familiar to her does not, it is worth noting, diminish its psychological veracity. That this subject chose to reveal herself through this particular literary vehicle rather than through some other suggests that the plot has particular meaning to her—which is precisely why her story is such a faithful rendition of the novel. The figures depicted in the card trigger, quite unconsciously, the reawakening of childhood issues that still require resolution. The story itself is a taking-off point for Sonya's projections and is important for that reason. It is an unconscious but very telling reflection of her psychological reality at the time of the story telling.

Notes

1. I call her perceptions mistaken because the older character in the card is not uncommonly described as benign. Details of the drawing do not have "weird" or "grimacing" connotations for all. William E. Henry, in fact, reported receiving interpretations of this card from women over the age of seventy in which the older woman was a "gently smiling and helpful person"; see *The Analysis of Fantasy: The Thematic Apperception Technique in the Study of Personality* (New York: Robert E. Krieger, 1973), 255.

2. The threat of old age is prominent in stories of middle-aged women, whereas fear of control by an older woman is prominent of stories of younger women; see Henry, *The Analysis of Fantasy*, 255.

7
Hidden Treasures

T he advice to know oneself is as old as philosophy or possibly even older, since one sage among the many to whom the dictum, "know thyself," was ascribed was a mythical Greek poetess who predated Homer. Although credit for its pithy wisdom has been given to the most renowned thinkers of ancient Greece (Plato, Pythagoras, Solon and Socrates, among others) and to all manner of wise people who came afterward, the advice is all but impossible to follow. We cannot know ourselves, not really, not fully. Our most determined attempts to be rational, objective observers of ourselves are impeded by unconscious forces to which the inner eye is blind.

No one was more aware of this than Sigmund Freud, who led the way to uncovering the hidden psychic forces, of the intrinsic limits to self-knowledge. The ideal but unattainable goal of psychoanalysis is "to make the unconscious conscious," he observed, and went on to develop a theoretical system that would narrow the gap between the ideal and the practical.

Working with the benefit of these and subsequent theories and constructs, it was possible for this research project to uncover answers to separation questions that could not come from conscious responses to direct inquiries, for the matters I and my assistants wished to measure were likely to be unknown to the subjects themselves. The indirect route we used, through the unconscious thought processes involved in generating fantasies, turned up an amazing wealth of hidden information.

Just how much of the unconscious lives of the subjects seeped through in their exercises in creative expression is better illustrated than described, and is illustrated best by an examination and analysis of the entire sequence of responses offered by a subject or two. Let us begin with the series of imaginings that Marie came up with when she was asked to describe the SIS scenes.

Marie

From the earlier introduction to two of her stories, it is clear that Marie sees the world as unloving and ungiving, and sees herself as forced to take from others. The protagonist limned in the stories she offered in response to cards 1 and 3 express her own feelings of resentment and self-absorption: "... resentment at being held there ..." and "very prissy, ... very worried about what the world thinks about her."

These utterances are not accidental. The main character speaks for Marie, out of whose life experiences, actual and perceptual, she is conceived. Marie's protagonist thinks the way she does because Marie thinks that way. Why does she think like this? What else do her stories tell us?

Card 2 Response

About the family scene shown on card 2 (resembling figure 2), Marie had this to say:

> Why this is almost the typical thing of "I'm so much better than they are." There is my family or my friends tilling the soil or back still doing the things they used to do, and I'm going to school, and I'm going to make something much better of myself; I'm not going to do this. I don't need them.

In the way she constructs this story, Marie epitomizes the fragmented or split self (level III). One part of herself becomes the young girl who, as the object of Marie's narcissistic projections, is the central focus of the tale: witness the recurring "I'm going to do this" and "I'm not going to do that." The protagonist, like Marie (who has no conscious sense of this trait in herself), has a clear sense of superiority: "I'm so much better than they are."

Although the main character is clearly defined, she fails to interact with other people who are, in fact, barely and dimly perceived. The fact that the other figures in the representation are simply lumped together as an undefined "they" suggests that other people (that is, all the *non-Maries* in the world) do not have psychological significance for her, but her remark about being "so much better than they are" implies that others may embody "ego alien" aspects of her self (parts of herself that are internally unacceptable). In that case, being close to others incurs the risk of exposing her own inadequacies, a risk that a precariously formed self can ill afford to take. Consequently, she must deny and disown her vulnerabilities, which is exactly what Marie is doing when she refuses to acknowledge her own neediness and inferiority: "I don't need them;" "I'm so much better."

The symbolic representation of a divided self is reinforced by the story's ending, which describes the girl as having no desire to return to her home. The creation of the apparently unbridgeable gulf between the protagonist and others parallels the gulf between parts of her self. The protagonist sees herself forging ahead on a solitary path. All narcissistic personalities ultimately make their way alone.

When it came to evaluating the different dimensions within levels, Marie's card 2 story received a total of 12 points because it captures the essence of level III in the divided self. It features these characteristic level III attributes:

III. 1—people perceived as undifferentiated   3 points
III. 2—splitting or idealization   3 points
III. 3—rejection of mother   3 points
III. 4—lack of interaction between characters   3 points

Although the clear definition of the protagonist argued for extra points (it is a V.1 trait), the possibility of reaching a higher level was effectively negated by the lack of definition of the other figures and by the overall tone of the story.

Card 4 Response

Moving on to the intimate scene depicted on card 4 (figure 4), Marie gave this response:

> I don't know if those are two men or a man and a woman. Evidently it is a woman. She seems to have fingernail polish on. A moment of commiseration, tenderness. Two people who seem to know each other well and are helping each other through some kind of trial. That is the feeling I have looking at this picture. As though he is comforting her, and she is trying to do the same for him.

An ironic aspect of psychoanalytic process is that what is left in the dark by being unsaid sometimes sheds light on unconscious matters, including separation issues. Not unlike other subjects, Marie fails to tell a narrative story in relation to this card but describes instead a vague and amorphous experience that includes the sensation of contentment and nurturance. A more separated woman might impose her own internal structure on the task by supplying missing details or by speculating about the nature of the "trial" alluded to by Marie. She, however, isolates the moment and has nothing to say about the events that may have led up to it.

What she does do is present an idealized relationship in which there is a perfect meshing of needs, a construction that denies the real possibility that anything untoward can happen. Indeed, the happy ending masks Marie's own real concern about losing someone close to her, specifically her husband.

But while she avoids, through denial, the pain of separation and loss, she nonetheless enjoys the sensuality of the picture. This pleasure may reflect the capacity to enjoy close physical contact, which, in turn, implies a degree of separation, because she is sufficiently separate to risk losing herself in another person. For Marie, in fact, this picture may express a dream wish fulfilled: to merge with another person and thereby ward off harm. If this is so, does the picture represent the child's magical wish for union or the culmination of the lifelong task of separation? In Marie's case, I incline towards the former.

Applying the SIS scale to Marie's story about card 4 resulted in 14 points and a compromise scoring at level IV. Basically, the story:

> III. 1—has undifferentiated characters   3 points
> III. 2—splits or idealizes people   3 points
>   But is ambiguous about:
> III. 3—nurturance
> III. 4—intimacy
>   So alternate point allocations were made for:
> V.3—acceptance of dependency   4 points
> V.4—existence of relationship   4 points

Further discussion of the scoring rationale for this story is included in the appendix at the end of this book.

Analysis

What Marie reveals about herself in her thinly veiled fictions holds promise for continuing growth. Her responses are consistently in the level III–IV range. Her ego strength, shown by her unredeemed contrariness, gives evidence that she was not psychologically crushed by her mother. She may, in fact, one day be able to love her mother—in her absence—because of her own move toward a firm, substantial self.

In sharp contrast with Estelle (who unconsciously confuses herself with her daughter in offering a clarification of a marriage proposal as intended "for the younger one, I mean," in response to card 3), Marie is always crystal clear about who she is. In the manner of pathological narcissists, she is certain of her own significance. Psychoanalyst Otto Kernberg, writing about the etiology of narcissism, described a dynamic that might explain her certainty. In such women, the ideal self (that is, the overinflated view of the self) and the real self (that is, the actual self) may merge regressively with the ideal object (that is, the idealized view of the parent) after the early stabilization of ego boundaries.[1] This is to say that the clear view that such a woman has of her "self" may be at considerable variance from the self that others perceive.

Rachel

Though narcissistic, Marie is much further along in personal development than is her associate in the study, Rachel, whose stories evidence serious personality problems. Rachel has trouble with control (she cannot confine the events in her stories to the individuals shown in the pictures) and even has momentary lapses in which she mistakes herself for her mother, suggesting the permeable ego boundaries of the borderline personality. Persons without solid ego boundaries typically lack the self-discipline and continuity of self in time and space that are required for perseverance at any given task for very long. Borderline personalities, for this reason, usually do not stay long in treatment that does not offer immediate and continuing gratification.

From her very first story Rachel shows herself to be in constant danger of being overwhelmed by her chaotic inner world. Primitive impulses are systematically thwarted in her original response to card 1—the mother-daughter scene of figure 5-1—and the mother dominates all her subsequent stories. In card 1, the daughter is first deprecated for her arrogance and grandiosity ("What is good enough for her mother is not good enough for her") and eventually punished as the girl with "the high-flying dreams" and "big plans" ends up "no better off" than her mother. The girl in the story almost becomes her mother as she replicates her life by marrying "a man just like her father" and being "no better off." In the process, the girl serves to express Rachel's desire to control the mother from within—as in projective identification—and to embody her inadmissible impulses of lust and greed.

Card 2 Response

Mother's sphere of influence is everywhere in Rachel's stories. Emotional entanglements with mothers are central to her response to card 2. Mother dominates, eventually even takes over the household, and the heroine's struggle to free herself from this enmeshment is both short-lived and futile. Here is the entire story:

> I see a man who is obviously a farmer, in ancient times, and a woman with a book who doesn't do any field work. What strikes me is that the young girl and the man have their backs to one another. These two fell in love and the young woman, who holds a Bible, is sort of separated—because her father did not do farm work.
>
> And the mother of the man who watches it does not interfere— does not take sides. I would say this woman will leave her husband (they have nothing in common) and the young woman goes back to her own folks—and the mother takes this opportunity to take over the household, and everything is the way it was before they got married.

The theme of the powerful mother dominates the story to such an extent that the young girl, who is the nominal heroine, is sufficiently alienated from the family she has just joined that she surrenders and goes "back to her own folks." Both mothers win; only the girl loses. She is caught in the immobilizing tension between her dependency needs (which urge her to stay) and her fear of self loss through engulfment (which tempts her to leave).

The crux of the paradox in which the heroine is caught is that having no intimate relationship (by leaving and being on her own) is tantamount to nonexistence. She cannot go and cannot stay. Whether her very apparent sense of alienation (she is "sort of separated," having come from a different environment wherein her father "did not do farm work") derives from her fear of loss of a tenuous self or from primitive dependency, her behavior implies a lack of differentiation between self and object. This is why Rachel empathizes in self-destructive ways with the enemy/mother or other persecutory objects (as is common for level II.2).

Since "mother" is everywhere in her world (the ambiguous reference to "the mother" in Rachel's story—obscuring the identity of the mother in question—confirms this), there is no escape. The protagonist (standing in for Rachel) capriciously drops love objects, or returns to earlier need-gratifying objects (mother) when those of more recent vintage (husband) cease to provide gratification, but none of these stratagems work to establish the sought-after sense of balance and control. It is worth noting that the way that Rachel, the borderline personality, described her protagonist as being outside the family circle is a dramatic departure from the common plots inspired by this card.

Excluding herself or others from interpersonal relationships permits the borderline person to overcome her sense of powerlessness by controlling a capricious world. The manner in which the story transcends the picture elements suggests a lack of emotional control and integration that is characteristic of level II.1. The characters, portraying aspects of the storyteller, seem to run away with the plot while their creator stands by helplessly, unable to save them, or herself, from their mutual and inevitable destiny.

Within the SIS frame of reference, Rachel's story about card 2 earned 8 points by fulfilling all level II criteria, and it exemplifies the true nature of the fluid self. It features these characteristics:

II.1—the teller gets carried away with the story-telling task	2 points
II.2—the attempt to control mother from within by sharing her greatness/power	2 points
II.3—the desire to be rid of mother (expressed in the brief marriage of heroine; cleavage of mother into good mother/husband and bad mother-in-law who takes over)	2 points
II.4—alternately clinging and withdrawing actions of heroine	2 points

The mother theme runs through Rachel's story about card 1 as well, with the mother now orchestrating the child's life to the point that the "earthy and practical mother" spares the daughter from "the worst" fate imaginable. Again, in describing the women pictured in card 3, the mother becomes a shadow who acts in the present.

The symbolism cannot be clearer. Rachel's stories manifest both her inability to free herself from her mother's domination and her underlying reluctance to cut the ties that continue to bind her. The psychoanalytic truth may well be that Rachel does not want to be free. Her resistance to freedom from her mother has ancient roots that are revealed in the lightly disguised oedipal (more accurately, pre-oedipal) content of her response to card 1. The incestuous wish for the father that is implied in "daughter much prettier than mother" and "spared the worst" is both punished ("she is no better off") and allowed partial gratification (she marries the "father").

Being free would require Rachel to surrender her old oedipal desires, if in fact she had them. Psychoanalysis, admittedly still more art than science, currently has some theorists who suggest the possibility that the oedipal and pre-oedipal stages are abridged in borderline personalities like Rachel, who in effect see their life stories in terms of dyads rather than the more conventional triads. For them, there is only one Other. Under this theory, the oedipal elements referred to here would be reinterpreted as indications of a secondary desire to have father only as a means of gaining greater intimacy with mother, the primary love object.

Card 3 Response

Without attempting to bring the oedipal issue to resolution, let us take time out for a systematic examination of Rachel's remaining stories. We can learn much about the most important one, the one that Rachel unconsciously tells about herself while describing the pictures. About card 3, Rachel says:

> Hmmmm. This is difficult. Apparently a young woman and an ugly old woman behind her. If you look close there is a similarity, even though one is pretty and the other ugly. I would say the old woman is the alter ego to the young woman. I would prefer to call it a shadow, which is what Henry James, no, William James called it. It might be what she is when she is old, but it also acts in the present; of what we all might be afraid. If this shadow remains with her, then it will be a negative influence, unless she finds ways of overcoming this negative attitude.

Card 4 Response

Rachel observes about the embrace scene on card 4:

> Well, I would say the present state is two people very much in love
> with each other. Not young people—married for some time. Have
> had their difficulties. Woman is strong willed and not as submis-
> sive as she looks on this picture. Now that they're more mature
> they have a lot in common and do love each other. And he begins
> to understand it is easier for the woman to be submissive and
> feminine if it is not demanded or expected of her. And she thanks
> him for that, making it easy for her to sort of correspond to the
> image he has of her.

Card 5 Response

And about the boat scene resembling card 5 (figure 5), Rachel says:

> I see a picture of a wooded area with a boat and I think it is spring.
> Atmosphere is very serene. Lovely. And there are no people. I can
> imagine there is a house close to the river, and the people moved
> away, and they don't use the boat anymore. And the boat looks out
> on the river and dreams of the good old days when children
> jumped into it, and now it is forgotten. And before long, it will
> become—it will rot—but it will become part of the whole scene.
> And nobody will ever know that there was a little boat that carried
> joyful children down the river.

Analysis

Nostalgia, wittiness, sadness, and more. Knowing nothing about Rachel
(and bear in mind that the tests were administered and analyzed with no
greater knowledge of Rachel's life than has been presented here) beyond
what is told in her stories, one can find in them the echoes of the pervasive
theme of her life. The repeated attempts of her characters to disentangle
themselves from maternal figures, alternating with furtive tries at rapprochement, are born out of Rachel's long domination by her mother, now
deceased. Not at all surprisingly, the protracted longing for her mother, the
longing to merge with her mother, interferes substantially with Rachel's
ability to be herself. It is difficult for her to differentiate her own thoughts
and feelings from those of other people.

   Examples of this "slippage" show up in her surrender to the mother,
disguised as a domineering husband, in her response to card 4, and in her
description of the two figures in card 2 who, reflecting different aspects of

her own self, run away with the plot, completely out of the control of their creator.

The magnitude of the problem is suggested by the degree to which Rachel's stories feature sacrifice of personal freedom and authenticity. Rachel indicates lack of ego strength and great vulnerability to outside influences in her repeated willingness to shift her stance with each picture, as if she is swept away by the visual stimuli instead of exercising free choice. The entire sequence demonstrates how stimulus-bound Rachel is. Note that, throughout her stories:

The locus of control lies outside rather than inside Rachel herself

Her boundary problems cause her to focus on the mother, whether the mother figure is the foreground or background of the pictorial representation

In the early stories, Rachel's abdication of household rule to the mother reveals empathy with her enemy (the persecutory object), reflecting her own willingness to knuckle under to authority to save herself from harm

In card 4, she shifts her stance by identifying with the passive side of the man; chameleonlike, she colludes in belittling herself by being eager enough to mold herself into his image of her that she thanks him for the privilege

In card 2, her characters move beyond her control and threaten to run away with the plot

It is also worth noting that without recourse to any overt acts of hostility, the punishments meted out for inappropriate behavior increase in severity in the sequence actually viewed by Rachel, so that:

In card 2, the mother restrains herself entirely from interfering and simply stands aside, letting the girl act on her own impulses and manage her way back to safety—there has been no gain and no loss: "everything is the way it was before"

Card 1 has the girl suffering her first defeat—by having her grandiose dreams burst amid a reality of being "no better off" than her mother

In card 4, the cycle is complete as the girl capitulates totally to the man, having in order to please him distorted herself to such an extent that she loses all sense of who she is

Moreover, the sequence hints at the reservoir of guilt and remorse that Rachel feels over her own "crimes" against her parents, those unconscious and unconscionable crimes of wishing to possess one parent and eliminate the other. In the mind of the unsophisticated child, the wish is equal to the deed. When a child's development is slowed by external forces, as Marie's was by parental overprotection and as Rachel's was by the lack of parental affection, the child falls prey to her own imagination. Lacking adequate opportunity to assess the magnitude of her misdoings against reality, the child imagines herself to be bad and deserving of punishment. The ensuing sentence is carried out unconsciously. In Rachel's case, the guilt is forcing its way into consciousness.

Since the capacity to experience such feelings is associated with higher levels of development, the signs of guilt and remorse in Rachel's sequence suggest that efforts to integrate earlier more primitive modes are beginning to work for her. The narratives move from the narcissistic exhibitionism of the stories related to cards 2 and 1 and the docile submission to the man in card 4, to more highly developed consideration of the mother-daughter relationship in card 3 and to the direct approach to separation and aging issues in the story of card 5. Somewhere along the way, Rachel seems to have recognized that holding on to her infantile wish for her mother's exclusive attention diminishes her.

There are, in all of this, some hopeful signs. Hostility is not given active expression. Despite her often verbalized protestations to the contrary, Rachel improves her story telling with practice. Her later stories stay more appropriately within the established boundaries; they are also more optimistic in tone. Rachel even hints at wishing to separate from the mother in the last sentence of the story describing card 3: that "if the shadow remains with her, then it will be a negative influence, unless she finds ways of overcoming this negative attitude."

With all these factors to take into consideration, the stories Rachel told led me, in the natural course of events, to make some educated guesses as to the current status and the future course of her development. This was my combined diagnosis/prognosis at the time of her first interview:

1. Defenses that have provided relief from disintegration anxiety are eroding, making way for renewed struggle with the mother issue. Rachel's denial of deep longing for her mother will yield to the stronger presence of the reapproaching mother.

2. Mature insistence on punishment for narcissistic exhibitionism paves the way to appropriate conduct and budding integrative efforts.

3. Risk taking (for example, losing mother, engaging in self-criticism) becomes possible with the acquisition of a firmer self. Rachel can move on once she is filled up with enough mothering.

At the time of the original testing, Rachel was clearly at a crossroad. Although she measured as a "fluid self" on the various tests, I concluded that she was close to choosing the road to greater maturity. I was pleased to find that expectation confirmed the next time we met, on the occasion of . a follow-up interview a year and a half later.

Note

1. Otto F. Kernberg, *Object Relations Theory and Clinical Psychoanalysis* (New York: Jason Aronson, 1976), 151.

8
The Story behind the Stories of Rachel

Describing her reaction to her mother's death five years before, Rachel said, "I actually became her for about a year." Expression of intense grief through vivid identification with the loved-and-lost one is not unusual, especially in the early stages of mourning, and may even be predictable for someone like Rachel, our exemplar of the "fluid self." She was at the time of the study experiencing considerable difficulty both in separating and in functioning.

No criticism of a fascinating woman is intended by this classification, which was based on her test scores and on the life history she herself presented. The very fact that she recognized and identified the latent ego boundary problems activated by her mother's death was a hopeful sign, suggesting a capacity for introspection that might lead to an eventual breakthrough once the difficult days of the recovery period ended. It has since become altogether clear that her poor functioning on the test was closely related to her protracted struggle to come to terms with an irrevocably motherless life.

There is more to Rachel's saga than has yet been told. After all the attention that has been devoted to the content and latent meaning of her creative responses to the SIS cards, the reader may have wondered whether there is any resemblance between the real person out of whose imagination they came and the hypothetical Rachel developed out of the analyses. Wonder no more. There is a real Rachel whom I have interviewed in depth (I know more about her than other subjects because she was seen twice), and presenting a fuller view of the person behind the stories is a feasible task.

It is also a necessary undertaking if the speculative insights previously offered without reference to Rachel's real life situation (except for the stipulated prior death of her mother) are to be validated. The facts of her life, as gathered from her case history, furnish the only possible reality check. With allowances for some subjectivity on her part in relating her life story and some on mine in perceiving her account, this, then, is an introduction to the "real" Rachel, as she revealed herself to me.

Initial Impressions

Rachel is a sixty-year-old woman who lives with her considerably older husband in a middle-class New York apartment. She enjoys good health and a life centered on her job, her unmarried son, and a number of growth-enhancing activities. Her appetite for learning and self-discovery is fed by voracious reading and by her long-standing membership in a mind-expanding therapy group. Her marital relationship has deteriorated to a secondary level of significance in her life. Only financial considerations now keep the marriage intact. By mutual decision, a situation apparently satisfactory to Rachel, she and her husband go their own ways.

Rachel is anything but reticent. I learn all the salient facts about her life quickly because she talks quickly. But I learn from more than her words. Let me interrupt her life story to describe my professional impressions of this woman during our first meeting.

An attractive, youthfully dressed woman who looks considerably younger than I know her to be, Rachel bubbles with delight at the prospect of expressing her ideas without hindrance. She rejects instantly the notion of meeting at her home where her husband "might try to get into the act." I suspect that she is herself adept at scene stealing, judging by the colorful clothes decorating her willowy figure, the blond hair piled high on her head, and the effervescent style with which she takes command.

Roles are fluid and interchangeable from the outset. She has me playing "mother" to her "daughter." Rachel is alternately coy and winning, inappropriately self-disclosing and resistant to my questions. She establishes her own agenda, propelling the interview along with repeated bids for my attention. Is this the recreation of a familiar and therefore unthreatening scenario, perhaps exacerbated by her recent loss?

Although her manipulations are clearly a test to see who is in charge, Rachel also seems to be asking for appropriate guidelines. I let her know gently that we are under time constraints as I draw the interview to a close, wondering to what extent her ego is bolstered by this entire experience—and how much bolstering it requires.

Rachel's Life Story

Rachel's psychic separation from her husband is not as big a problem for her as it might be had not early and hard lessons taught her about traveling alone along life's roads. She was born in 1924, the only child of a middle-class family in pre-Hitler Germany. Her mother was a teacher and, according to Rachel, "a social charmer with animal magnetism who was loved by everyone." Despite her best efforts, the child felt unable to please her mother with her appearance, her behavior, or her aptitude.

Nor did she do better with her father, an introverted, reclusive art history professor whose energies and enthusiasm were restricted to his professional interests. As far as his daughter could tell, only his scholarly pursuits and his books mattered to him. She could not impress him if she tried. "But I didn't try very hard," she reports.

Rachel characterizes herself as an adventurous but not very ambitious child, taken by her parents to be both undisciplined and stupid. The two had devoted their lives to education and, having successfully taught the children of others, were immensely frustrated at their inability to teach their own daughter anything of value. She became the embodiment of "all their bad projections."

Her earliest memory features her father in a nurturing role: "I was sitting in a buggy and my parents—who looked like giants—were eating bread and jam. I was aware of being cute, and my father responded the most. He was the one actually eating the bread."

His early response to her "cuteness" served to establish a lifelong pattern: attempts at charm and coyness became Rachel's means for seeking forgiveness, special favors, and love. As long as she was cute, she soon learned, all else would be forgiven—especially her femaleness. Like most men of his place and time, Rachel thinks, her father believed women to have no other mission than that of being beautiful enough to attract men.

The forces of history intersected with intrafamiliar dynamics when Rachel was eleven. Adolph Hitler's rise to power in Germany soon meant that anyone with Jewish blood, or anyone married to someone so "tainted," was considered a menace to the state. Rachel's father, who was not Jewish, was demoted to a lowly teaching position. If Rachel's recollection is to be trusted, he bemoaned only the loss of income he required to support his scholarly interests.

Her mother, whose maternal grandfather had been Jewish, was summarily dismissed from her teaching post so that the legacy of her Jewish inheritance "would not poison the souls of Germany's children." Devastated by the dismissal—"teaching was her whole life"—and by the depths to which her "bad blood" had brought her family, the mother released her frustrations by shaming her daughter. She belittled Rachel before others, speaking of her as if she were not present: "Just listen to her! Isn't she stupid?" she would say. She sometimes had fits of hysteria during which she engaged in bizarre behavior that occasionally had her "rolling on the floor and yelling"; the presence of Rachel's friends did not deter her from these performances.

As Rachel grew into adolescence, her mother's "attacks" intensified, and the girl stopped bringing her friends home. She saw Mother as an embarrassment who "needed to be in the center no matter where she was." Mother acted out inappropriately and immaturely, becoming fiercely competitive when Rachel began to date young men. She acted more like a peer and even a rival than a mother.

The parenting that Rachel failed to get from her parents fortunately was supplied by a succession of devoted nurses and governesses who were hired to raise her. They fostered her own sense of self and let her feel good about being different from her parents. From them she learned indirectly how to protect her own emerging self by refusing to become like either parent. She knew that she would be different.

She *was* different and so conscious of her "difference" that she had no expectation of ever being like them. "I was a misfit," she says, "but a nice misfit. I felt instinctively that I was all right in spite of everything." These instincts and positive feelings about herself became part of her survival armor. She developed ways to defend herself against parental tyranny, adopting passive-aggressive behaviors as part of a warped but effective form of self-assertion.

"I never fought them openly, with my elbows," she recalls now, chuckling at her deviousness. She actively avoided tasks that she disliked performing and stayed out of view, and then, "I simply disappeared."

Her strategic evasion of parental scrutiny worked sporadically until eventually her parents again took notice of her and of her failures to live up to their exacting standards. Then bursts of explosive anger ("which I deserved," she notes) were directed at the child. She adopted a tough "I don't care" stance, and no one seemed to notice that beneath the protective layers of toughness and bravado was a hurt child who could not show her pain, not even to herself. Her ignorance of this pain turned out to be both her salvation and her undoing.

She stayed with her parents until she was almost thirty. A self-acknowledged "late bloomer," she became suddenly impatient to make a new life for herself. Recognizing the need to separate herself from her parents "in order to grow," she emigrated to the United States. The physical separation proved easier to attain than the emotional separation as she struggled to find herself in a new country.

Like the rapprochement child whose physical prowess outstrips his emotional readiness to separate, Rachel tackled projects beyond her scope and then suffered the pain of defeat. She now recognizes the deep fear and insecurity that underlay her attempts at independent living. She admits to "still very much wanting [a] father." It was not long before she found one: a much older man who fostered the illusion that she would be "protected spiritually and emotionally."

"I felt safe with my husband-to-be," she says, stunned now at her earlier naiveté. The marrige was unhappy from the beginning, although the courtship that led up to it started, romantically enough, with a conflict between two suitors. Rachel tells the story with relish.

"One of the men, the manager of a food chain and my employer, was just the kind my parents would have loved." He shared their materialistic values and "was German on top of it." But he was tricky. Reports Rachel, "He wanted me to overhear him negotiating his financial affairs, imagining I would marry him if I learned how well off I would be [when he died]." But Rachel, who had her own tricks up her sleeve, took a look at a bank officer and decided to go out with him instead, not because she found him irresistible but to annoy her employer.

"I did all kinds of things to aggravate him," she says, seeming to take pleasure in thwarting the desires of others in much the same way that she perceived her own childhood desires to have been constantly thwarted. Still, she reports herself to have been "very much captivated" by the bank officer. He reminded her of the positive aspects of her German upbringing and shared her father's cultural orientation. Also, like her father, he was creative and shared Rachel's interest in literature and the theater. She married him.

With the deep void in Rachel's psyche to contend with, the marriage was in trouble from the start. Disillusionment set in before the first year was over. But while the glow faded from her marital relationship, she was able to maintain the semblance of a marriage. Family, and the appearance of family, was always important to Rachel. One needed family to be sure of oneself. She continued to visit her parents faithfully until they both died, all the while scrupulously building a new family for herself in the United States. She needed to belong. When the relationship with her husband, Paul, failed to fulfill her needs, she set about establishing a more gratifying relationship with her son. Soon after Michael was born, when she was in her late thirties, Rachel found justification for isolating the boy from his father.

"He did the most terrible thing a parent can do," she says, describing Paul's failure to keep promises he had made to the child. She responded by setting up situations, including extended vacations from which Paul was excluded, in which she and Michael could explore the world without his father. If she exacerbated by this behavior whatever problems did exist, she seems to be blissfully devoid of guilty feelings.

She does recognize that she may be "too close" to Michael who, at twenty-five, has just recently moved from the family home. A perennial architecture student, he has yet to graduate from college. She encourages his academic and artistic pursuits, even paying for his classes, and goes a step further. She enrolls in classes of mutual interest along with Michael and thereby reinforces their relationship of mutual dependence.

She admits to being "more of a companion than a mother," just like her mother before her. It comes as no surprise to learn that Michael's attachment to young women have been "on and off affairs," mostly "off" I would guess. But it is the young women who defer making long-term commitments while he reportedly seeks the sort of close attachment that only his mother has been able to manage with him.

Rachel had no other child. Indeed, involved as she was in the one, she had no need of a second. Deciding that her uterus was "very beaten up" by her one pregnancy and labor, both "difficult," she underwent a hysterectomy at the age of thirty-eight, and the issue was settled. She felt no detectable sorrow (or hid her sorrow from herself). It was easier to deal with one child.

In fact, dyadal relationships were always more comfortable than triadal relationships for Rachel. Recollections of her childhood are largely in "mother and me" terms, only occasionally focusing on "father and me." In her marriage, the threatening triad was eliminated by her exclusion of her husband Paul from the nuclear family circle. The old adage about two being company and three a crowd was never more assiduously incarnated.

A Spiritual Search

Her mother's death brought Rachel face-to-face with the questions that religions seek to answer and thus renewed an already active quest for a true spiritual center. Raised as a nominal member of the German Lutheran Church, she was no more of a practicing Christian than her parents or their parents before them had been. Familial allegiance to the church was largely a matter of convenience—though the matter raised to life-and-death significance as long as Jewish blood was an issue in Nazi Germany.

Nonetheless, Christianity had given her warm feelings about a loving "father" who cared for her and protected her. She longed to embrace the "mother" church for comfort, but, appalled by its authoritarian doctrine and by the "bigots" who adhere to such doctrine, she wrestled with the same kind of love-hate that she had felt toward her mother and father, and, later on, her husband. She looked for a more comfortable religious home.

At about the time that her father died, Rachel took a job running a gift shop in a Unitarian church. Being in that religious climate served her needs for the next ten years until an emotional entanglement related to her mother's death forced her back into religious limbo, as well as into unemployment. Not long afterward, while still emotionally raw, she accepted a temporary job as a faculty assistant at a school connected with the Lutheran Church ("father's church"). The job reawoke her earliest religious misgivings, and she found herself desperately unhappy in the Lutheran environment. She left her job, by mutual agreement, and renewed her quest for religious sanctuary.

After some study and reflection, she determined that she would feel comfortable within Judaism. She once more found a position at the center of her newly adopted family, working now as the receptionist at a Jewish community center. Helped by occasional calls to assist in the center's child care groups, she is again able to imbue her new family with magical properties that protect her against the ravages of the secular world. This time, the magic seems to be working; no personal drama has yet taken this job from her.

The emotional upheavals associated with these changes show the level at which Rachel's development is fixated—or to which she has temporarily regressed. In each instance, the religious institution and/or its representatives stand for unassimilated parts of herself. She has tried, from middle adulthood on, to fill the structural void within her by defining such persons as substitute parents whose positive attentions could reinforce her sense of self. While these idealized relationships lasted, she experienced herself as worthwhile, but when, despite her hunger to merge with her gods, she inevitably found defects that forced her to sever her ties with them, her inner emptiness prevailed.

In retrospect, the abandoned persons/institutions signify only pain and trouble for Rachel. When Rachel was first interviewed, the suffering that accompanied her departure from the Unitarian church setting was fresh in her mind, but she was still quite far from understanding the real cause for her pain. Despite the fact that her job termination followed the death of her mother by a few short weeks, Rachel's account apparently misses the causal connection between the two events.

This is how she explained her leaving: "I was having problems with the dean of the Unitarian school, who, of course, reminded me of my father. I felt like something was going to happen, if I did not get out of my job there—just like with my parents. It had something to do with rejecting the patriarchal god image."

She projected the residual yearning for God onto the dean himself. "He was a Ph.D., he was omnipotent, and he underwent a metamorphosis. God became man, you see, and I could not cope with that." Largely ignoring the role played by her own exotic religiosity, Rachel attributes her crisis to the dean's psychological problems. The problem was all due to the fact that "he had never developed his feelings—and he had very strong feelings for me which he could not handle."

Still blind to her unconscious collusion in the happenings, Rachel could not acknowledge the longings of her inner child. To cover up her deep disappointment and hurt, she saw the dean as being entirely at fault and herself as the poor victim, unfairly penalized. She was "slapped in the face" (dismissed from her job at the church) even though she had "given her all for this man."

The sequence of events, it turns out upon inquiry, started with the dean's attempt to console her after the death of her mother and moved quickly into an entanglement that was "something beyond our control." Her father, one will recall, had failed to meet her childhood demands for support when her mother became emotionally unavailable to her. Now, again seeking succor from a revered man, she permitted the establishment of a situation ripe for exploitation. She was no likelier to gain true consolation from the dean than from her own father.

The short-lived affair "happened gradually, of course"; it ended suddenly and left her in despair. Emotionally raw and vulnerable, she was still ruminating over the unfortunate turn of events a few months later when, working on the schedule of the Lutheran school, she used a semester break to travel to the mountains. There she had a religious experience, "just like Luther," that changed the course of her life.

"I was alone up there, and there was a terrible thunderstorm. Nobody in his right mind would have gone up there." [Implication: *I am not in my right mind.*] "It was dangerous." [*I am braver than most people.*]

Having purposefully put herself at risk in search of the Truth (with a capital *T*), Rachel received a vision of Martin Luther, who appeared as a "huge light, not quite as high as the wall in this room." Whether or not the spirit of Luther communicated with her Rachel does not recall. Evidently the vision itself, the experience of religious insight akin to Luther's own religious experiences, stunned her into senselessness. When she came to, she rationalized her own rebellion, determining never to return to her father's church. Without a thought for the paradox—that her final abandonment of the church was brought about by the spiritual intervention of the founder of that church—she left the job, which had never been right for her. Her admission that her departure was "sort of mutual, though," suggests awareness of her own contribution to the job's unsuitability. It was clearly someone closer to the scene than Martin Luther who agreed that the termination was a good idea.

With free time for reflection, Rachel moved toward the realization that something was wrong with her life. She spent unstructured days at home, passively following her impulses. She took to writing stories about her past (in the third person—the "observing ego"), mostly about her experience with the dean. Her own analyses, based largely on her knowledge of psychological theory, helped her achieve a measure of self-understanding.

Despite the difficulty of the self-discovery process—she observed herself becoming more and more depressed in the face of her own inadequacies and failings—she continued to seek self-knowledge, though hardly ever in the conventional fashion. She sought insight with a passion, determined to find her best self.

Psychological Rebirth

In search of a true revelation, Rachel enrolled for a nine-day miniworkshop and wilderness survival experience held in a desolate area of Montana under the leadership of an Indian chief and several therapists of the "est" persuasion. This event, which coincidentally (or not) opened on the fifth anniversary of her mother's death, started with grueling initiation rites (topped off with a totally naked immersion in ice water), followed by a week of high-pressure communal self-discovery sessions that culminated in a rigorous two-day exercise in coping with cold, hunger, and isolation.

Suffering through this final part of the workshop intensified her readiness for another "peak experience," another vision. Left alone without food on an island for two days of solitary combat with herself and with the forces of nature, Rachel quite realistically expected to get in touch with her inner voice or to collapse from the effort, relying on a rescue boat patrolling the shoreline nearby to avert disaster.

Stripped by design of all physical comforts and knowing how defenseless she would soon be, Rachel at first tried to avoid painful insights. Wanting to prolong the good feelings that had accrued from her sense of mastery over the wilderness around her, she went into isolation talking to herself, loudly rejecting the notion of experiencing another vision. But her attempts to look outward rather than inward—by simply exploring the limits of the island— came to an end on the second day when she was overcome with nausea, a clear sign to her that "something was pressing toward resolution."

Memories of her parents soon flooded her consciousness. Reluctantly, she accepted the realization that she had never truly mourned their loss. She thought of the circumstances surrounding their deaths and moved, in ever deeper sadness, to reflection on mortality in general. Death seemed everywhere around her. Morbid speculation consumed her psychic energies until she was no longer sure (she recalled later) whether she was dead or alive. "Maybe," she thinks now, "that's really how it is when you die. You just sit around and wait."

By the time the patrol boat came by on a routine check, she was unable to recognize the passengers although they had been her companions for the prior seven days. Nonetheless, she persuaded them that she was all right and sent them on their way. Alone again, she was deluged with guilt feelings. She wept copiously and set about building a memorial to her parents out of blocks of wood that she found nearby, "high up on a rock where it was safe."

Not far away, she came upon a depression in the ground, a "little hole" that "looked like a coffin." It is in a soft, childlike voice, that Rachel recounts her experience. "And I crept into my hole, and I slept, and I cried."

She awoke the next day feeling newly born. "I was a new person. I felt marvelous, and I did not want to leave, not even for a moment. But of course I had to!"

Analysis

This report of psychological rebirth occurring between interviews, was a turning point in her inner life, and provides a good opportunity to leave

Rachel's history for a short digression into a dynamic formulation of her story up to this stage of her life. The rest of her factual history will be examined after we look at the psychodynamic forces underlying the facts so far.

Rage at her mother is at the root of the emotional disturbances that interfered with Rachel's growth and clouded her life. Largely unnurtured and unprotected by her mother, and seriously thwarted in the expression of her true self, she felt alone in the world, a "misfit." She held on to her anger and pain to confirm her existence.

Only after extricating herself from her mother's power was Rachel able to live fully. When she finally achieved freedom from maternal influence—dramatically expressed in the ritual burial in which her own bad self dies along with her parents and her good self emerges as if "newly born"—she experienced a sense of rebirth. She was at last on the way to becoming mistress of her life. It was she, it becomes clear, rather than the dean who underwent metamorphosis.

Despite her rage, Rachel remained psychologically bound to her parents as long as she did because hurt feelings are preferable to the numbing deadness that was her alternative. (Recall that in Rachel's interpretation of card 2 fear of self loss immobilized the girl "who stays".) Her vulnerability to outside influence and lack of ego strength likewise explain her persistence in a loveless marriage and her unconscious readiness to be shunted about from Unitarians to Lutherans (this trait is parelleled by her willingness to shift her stance on each picture card).

The punishments meted out by her real and symbolic parents were perversely self-affirming, giving her weak self a proof of existing through a perversion of the Cartesian credo into something on the order of: "They respond; therefore, I am." She was able to achieve a limited sense of power and control over her own destiny by subconsciously provoking others to punish her. Through self-destructive acts, she sought to protect herself against the random attacks of her parents and from the unpredictable and terrifying world outside her doors. (Recall how in Rachel's story the girl in card 2 controls her suitor/husband and other "objects" by capriciously dropping them when they cease providing her with gratification.)

In the interest of survival, the young Rachel made costly emotional trade-offs. Ignoring her own unhappiness, she became insensitive to the feelings of others. Unable to experience the gratification of a fully reciprocal love relationship in her formative years, it became difficult for her to feel love. It took almost her full lifetime to rekindle in herself the loving feelings for her mother that resolution of her early deprivation required. Her anguish for the lost little girl she had been stood in her way.

Given the loveless childhood, further retreat into herself would not have been an unlikely escape had not important compensations in Rachel's experience provided some noteworthy ego protection. She apparently enjoyed much freedom to be what she termed "an adventuresome kid" despite what she perceived as endless demands from her parents. Further, the dedication of both parents to their professional interests and their abdication of most caretaking obligations to others gave Rachel access to loving caretakers who were able to compensate in part for parental rejection. Blending their affection with occasional positive strokes from her father, Rachel was able to plant the seeds of self-love beneath the surface of her childhood discontent.

Problems revolving around loving and being loved have wide ramifications. Since the child Rachel could not afford to love others, she became so wrapped up in herself that people and events in the outside world scarcely existed for her, despite her often articulated desire to be an integral part of that world. So tenuous is her connection with events outside herself that Rachel's account of her early life in Germany made no reference to the hardships caused by the war years or to the horrors visited upon innocents by the Nazi regime.

But in fairness to Rachel, one must consider other possible explanations for the selectivity of her recall: perhaps a degree of survival guilt (a guilt reaction to surviving a time and place that proved fatal to others) has compounded a repressed, paralyzing fear for her own safety that maintains its forcefulness, long after the threat has passed. Or, and this is just as likely, Rachel simply kept quiet about this part of her life because the frame of reference imposed by the interviewers simply did not bear directly on it. Like Holocaust survivors who are only now, some forty years afterward, speaking out about the horrors that they suffered or witnessed others suffering, Rachel may have terrible memories that she simply chose not to discuss. It would be doing her an injustice to imply, without direct investigation, that she has simply repressed all unpleasant memories of what happened around her during her many years in Nazi Germany.

In any case, I suspect that the internal threat of self loss and/or of parental loss was at least as terrifying to Rachel as any outside danger that could assault her juvenile imagination. Still, the existence of parallels between elements of her family life and elements of the Nazi era, especially in the analogous use of scrapegoats to carry undeserved burdens (in the one case, the burden of a shaky marriage, in the other, of a psychopathic society), may well have exacerbated her private fears.

The Theme of Maternal Rejection

Rachel wanted nothing more than she wanted her mother's love, but attaining that love was out of the question. In the child's eyes, Mother was such a paragon of perfection whom "everybody loved" that presuming to emulate her would have been inconceivably presumptuous. So Rachel settled for being different and for suppressing the pain of watching her mother lavish affection on the children of others.

Professional dedication to teaching was "Mother's whole life," perhaps in atonement for her unconscious rejective wishes toward her own daughter. Devoting herself single-mindedly to nurturing the children assigned to her, Rachel's mother may have assuaged the guilty feeling engendered by her exclusion from nurturance of the child born to her. In any case, Rachel felt deprived and was jealous.

She was also dubious about the explanation given for her mother's return to teaching soon after Rachel's birth. When she raised the question with her mother, years later, of course, when in her mature years she still brooded over her early deprivations, her mother justified the return to work with economic reasons. She had wanted to assure her pension rights, she said, implying that her preference would have been to care for her baby. That implication flew in the face of Rachel's remembered resentments; she still sometimes complains that "everything, including nursing me, was done in a rush—not as it should be."

If Rachel sensed in early childhood (as she now knows) that she was an unwanted child, we can understand her frantic attempts to win her mother's love through attention-getting antics. This approach contrasts sharply with that used in a similar situation by Marie, who chose to develop competence in different areas in order to attract praise. But Rachel's early inference of being unwanted, far from being a paranoid delusion, was eventually corroborated by her mother, who casually referred to having blotched her attempts to avoid pregnancy by relying on crude contraceptive measures and, to add (perhaps without intending to) to the humiliation the news would have on her listener, made light of a subsequently bungled abortion attempt.

Once born, Rachel had been a wanted child, her mother asserted, but despite Rachel's wholehearted desire to believe her, the unconvincing and delinquent assurance could not undo the pain caused by the other maternal revelations. They were difficult for Rachel to absorb. She did not, indeed, volunteer any of this information. It was during my review of the test results and notes on the first interview that it occurred to me that Rachel had been unwanted and that her mother had experienced some guilt over this.

Rachel's attention-seeking during the test administration was the first clue. Quick confirmation of my hunch came from several test responses in which Rachel profoundly rejected mother/mothering and also had the story child actively showing off in order to capture maternal attention. These notions are not as contradictory as they may at first glance appear to be. It was altogether possible for Rachel to reject mothering out of fear of becoming her own "bad" mother while holding on to her primitive love for the "good" mother who had given her life.

There seemed also to be a meaningful parallel to her real life in that the mother in her SIS stories had an obsessive involvement with her daughter— suggesting the mother's need to make her over in order to deny rejective tendencies—while the girl lingered on in the household, in fear of being "abolished" by her. When I raised this emotionally charged issue with Rachel, she expressed surprise that I knew more than she had knowingly told me. It was then that she confirmed that she had felt unwanted and revealed that she had been unable to leave the parental home until she was more than thirty years old—just like the protagonist in her story to card 2.

While it may be theoretically possible for an unwanted child to win the love of its mother, the odds against it are substantial, and the love that overcomes the odds may in fact be too late to avert lasting damage. Truly wanting a child may well be a sine qua non for maternal satisfaction. Without this maternal desire, the relationship between baby Rachel and her mother was doomed from the outset. The infant became a painful reminder to the mother of her own deficiencies, as well as of the lack of love she herself had suffered as a child.

I say this because the available interview data suggests that Rachel's mother was also unwanted. In support of this hypothesis are the reports of her attention-getting hysterical episodes; her dissatisfaction with her own daughter; the intensification of her internal conflicts upon losing her nur- turant outlet, her work (which had allowed her to mother herself through mothering her charges); and the absence of fulfillment in her marital rela- tionship (Rachel, in thinking her to be sexually frustrated, missed the mark; more primitive needs were left unfulfilled by her mother's marriage). There is at least a hint in all this, which clearly cannot be substantiated, of yet another parenting problem somehow transmitted from generation to generation.

Whatever the story of the mother's birth, the deep ambivalence sur- rounding Rachel's birth explains, to some degree, Rachel's inability to draw nourishment and sustenance in her later years from the sort of reser- voir of mother love available to women raised in a generally loving atmos- phere. But if she was unable to subordinate her negative feelings entirely, Rachel's mother was nonetheless able to deal positively with the uncon- scious guilt that this situation engendered through constructive work. And though her attacks on Rachel escalated when the termination of her employment eliminated her primary mechanism for expiation and self- fulfillment, there were only isolated incidents of destructive behavior directed against the child.

There are other indications of positive maternal intentions, if not posi- tive parenting behavior, toward her child. That the child, once born, was important to her self-esteem is reflected in her continuing effort to transform Rachel into a model of perfection. A good child would be proof that she was a good mother, that she had not harmed her child by acting out destructively.

The child, correctly more interested in being than in being good, perceived the transformation attempt as a threat and began a defensive confrontation of wills that peaked in adolescence. Finally concluding that the price she had to pay for love was too high if it meant having her own spirit crushed, Rachel stopped trying to please and simply retreated into laziness, mental dullness, and impassivity. It was a difficult pattern to break. Indeed, she may never be free of the fear described by psychoanalyst Bruno Bettelheim that "her mother's unconscious would dominate her unconscious."[1]

Despite her vocal denials of wishes to follow in her mother's footsteps, Rachel could not divert herself totally from that path. How strongly Rachel actually identifies with her mother shows both in her SIS responses and in her life choices. She gave birth to one child, relatively late in life, and, like her mother, left the child in the care of others while she went out to earn a living. She shares her mother's intellectual interests, her gratifying involvement with children (at the community center), and perhaps her unconscious rejective tendencies as well.

There was one clear advantage to Rachel in her mother's forthrightness. She knew or suspected where she stood regarding this most important fact of her life and was therefore able to trust her own perceptions in other areas. The unequivocated truth is sometimes easier for a child to deal with than is pretense. No matter how painful, it is in some ways liberating.

The Broad Spectrum of Borderline Phenomena

More needs to be said about the borderline personality category into which I have several times, apparently casually, placed Rachel. Not unlike others, this psychological category is defined by highly imprecise boundaries within which can be found a bewildering amalgamation of psychotic, neurotic, and healthy elements. In fact, the borderline syndrome is used by clinicians to classify patients who simply do not fit in the traditional pigeonholes, whose mental processes are sometimes neurotic, sometimes psychotic, sometimes normal. Despite some learned attempts to authenticate the borderline personality as a distinct syndrome (marked, according to Kernberg, by "a specific condensation of pregenital and genital conflicts"[2]), the category serves, practically speaking, as a diagnostic shelter for the otherwise homeless inhabitants of the borderland between neurosis and psychosis.

All of this is nothing more than an attempt to explain the difficulty I had in classifying Rachel, whose symptoms occasionally overlapped with

Marie's. Unlike the classic borderline personality, Rachel can experience shame and guilt and can engage in the mourning process. We can say, in the psychoanalytic frame of reference, that she seems to have reached the (oedipal) phase of libidinal development even though her clinical picture still displays pregenital conflicts, which may not only come to the surface but actually dominate the clinical picture. Despite the common perception to the contrary, neurotic patients, who are not nearly as disturbed as borderlines, also have pregenital fixations. Or we can say, in simpler terms, that Rachel has a conscience contrasts with the borderline personality's characteristically impaired capacity for such concern and a highly blurred distinction between the ego and the superego (conscience).

Besides her capacity for experiencing a variety of affective states, Rachel thinks logically and employs higher level defenses, especially repression. She thus may have been able to repress, or eject from conscious awareness, memories of the childhood terrors that she must have experienced growing up in a war-torn country, especially one beset by such an extremely oppressive regime as that of the masters of terror that ruled Nazi Germany during her childhood.

Repression, which is strictly a function of the ego, is a defense not generally available to the borderline individual, whose ego is by definition weak or undeveloped. It takes a strong ego, accustomed to dealing with reality and with the demands of the superego, to repress terrifying memories and guilt-ridden impulses. So Rachel departed from the norm, if norm there is for borderline personalities, in this respect.

Rachel is further distinguished from other borderline personalities by her capacity for object relations. Her inner world is populated with whole objects that can have a "good" and a "bad" side, suggesting a degree of object constancy capable of sustaining the complex, triadic object relations of the oedipal phase. This is in contrast with the helter-skelter world typically displayed by borderlines on projective tests, a chaotic world in which people, or even body parts, merge with one another or with inanimate objects. On the basis of this trait, psychoanalyst Roy Grinker was moved to categorize the borderline personality as a *"sui generis* condition specifically characterized by deficient self and object constancy."[3] Rachel deviates from this norm as well.

Nonetheless, I believe that at the time she was tested, Rachel manifested a borderline personality organization, possibly a transient state associated with the loss of her mother since self/other boundaries are typically unclear following such losses. Borderline indications came early, when her first test responses to the SIS cards showed her yielding totally to the visual representations. Her loss of distancing led her to verbalize thoughts and speculations only tangentially related to the depictions. Sometimes she mistook her inner feelings for external perceptions of real events, to the extent that, perceiving herself in a setting dominated by the presence of death, she actually considered the possibility that she was herself dead.

The further corroboration of ego weakness provided by her recurrent visions is somewhat diluted by her apparent ability to distinguish consistently between her fantasy life and reality. The crucial question is this: Are the self-induced states that led her to doubt her very existence, to interpret a natural phenomenon as the image of Luther, to fail to recognize her friends after a short separation—are these states psychotic delusions (that is, false beliefs) or are they more normal illusions (that is, distorted perceptions)? The clinical reality testing conventionally used to separate psychotics from borderline individuals fails us here. We do not know enough about Rachel's solitary visionary experiences to evaluate them precisely. I took them, nonetheless, as borderline events.

Further indexes of borderline organization are found in the absence from her early history of any indications of shame and guilt (it took Rachel nearly a lifetime to mourn the loss of her mother's love) and the lack of the kind of signal or social anxiety that typifies higher developmental levels. Finally, her history exhibits the six salient characteristics ascribed by Gunderson and Singer to the borderline personality.[4] According to her own account, she has characteristically evidenced (1) intense affect, (2) impulsive behavior, and (3) brief psychotic episodes.

The remaining characteristics of the Gunderson and Singer borderline outline could also be discerned, though admittedly not without risk of subjective bias. Rachel's psychological tests indicated (4) a primitive personality organization (that is, a high animal percentage and a low structure score on the Rorschach). And her demeanor when first tested gave evidence of the fifth and sixth criteria, (5) transient relationships characterized by dependency, and (6) poor social adaptation.

According to Kernberg, discrepant findings such as were found in this case may be partially understood in relation to masochistic character organization.[5] A masochist may appear to be much more disturbed in her relationships and on psychological tests than she in fact is because, anticipating defeat and disaster, she unconsciously creates situations that cause trouble for her, in the manner of a self-fulfilling prophecy. Rachel's doomed search for the lost symbiotic relationship with a mother figure (embodied in the dean and others) meshes perfectly into the masochistic game plan.

It is little wonder that women like Rachel rarely achieve their goals even when the pursuit of those goals becomes the theme that dominates their lives. The Maries of the world somehow know how to satisfy their needs despite their own shortcomings; Marie enjoyed an exceptionally supportive marriage before her husband's illness, and she received love and admiration for her achievements. Lacking the self-protective and therefore self-isolating nature that often accompanies narcissistic character traits, borderline women, like Rachel at midlife, expose their vulnerable psyches to the cutting edges of the real world.

Some interesting work by Grinker confirms my classification.u Grinker categorized psychiatric patients in four groups, ranging from those individuals totally unable to establish relationships (group I) to those (group IV) who seek dependent, clinging relationships and who, lacking such relationships, fall into anaclitic depressions, often upon the loss of their mothers or others on whom they have depended. In the intermediate range, the group II subjects, whose behavior represents the core process, vacillate between moving toward and away from people; group III includes passive individuals who have all but given up their searches for identity.

Rachel seems to fit into group II, but group IV is in fact more suitable, both for her and for Marie, since this is the group that comes closest to the neurotic border (giving Rachel the benefit of the doubt). Unlike the patients in group I, who approach the psychotic border, or in group III, who despair of establishing meaningful relationships, these women continue to search for an element of fulfillment through interpersonal relations.

The fact that both women exhibited almost exclusively dyadic relationships is an intriguing one, since this defect in affectionate relationships is known to be developmental, requiring precipitating circumstances early in life. In both life accounts, these circumstances have been alluded to without systematic analysis. In Marie's case, the traumatic events that clouded all subsequent events are clearly defined. The dramatic and seemingly abrupt collapse of her sense of omnipotence occurred at around the time of her seventh birthday, when her sister was born and she felt her parents turning away from her.

The collapse was predictable. Her sense of grandeur had been built on shaky ground; early failure to resolve adequately the rapprochement crisis had blocked her ability to build up the reserves of healthy narcissism her life situation demanded. Until she was seven, she managed to defend her vulnerable ego with an alternative buildup of overarching grandiosity.

When the birth of her sister brought the weak structure tumbling down and the effectiveness of her defense to a sudden halt, the residual sense of grandiosity left her with an overinflated view of mother/self that was never reduced to realistic size; it became impossible for the real persons to match the mental image. To ease the narcissistic hurt of this dual rebuff, Marie invented the myth that she was special to her father, who replaced her mother in the central dyad. He became the mirror to her lost ideal state of self.

In Rachel's case, the rapprochement theme of the search for dyadic relations predominated because of earlier, more all-pervasive attacks on her self-esteem (which explains the fact that she regressed farther than Marie did). This caused her to hover around mother longer, restricting her access to the world, and creating a vicious circle in which her own frustrations caused her to frustrate her parents. In time, her narcissistic grandiosity was replaced by masochistic self-disparagement, but whole object relations remained dominant.

Recapitulation

Let us return now to Rachel's tale and to what we have learned from it, after this long aside on aspects of the borderline personality. We left her autobiographical account at the turning point to which she was brought by her mystical wilderness experience. We have seen her personality, to this stage in her life, shaped largely by these salient themes:

1. *Rage at her mother for failing to nurture.* This interfered with her growth and development, causing her to be drawn into a series of religious "families" and to remain in a loveless marriage. It also forced her to turn to her generally unresponsive father for nurturing.
2. *Self-affirming and self-destructive passive-aggression.* Ignoring the stated demands of her parents allowed her to control her destiny by unconsciously bringing about punishment.
3. *Insensitivity to herself and others.* Burying, in the interest of survival, her loving feelings toward her mother made it difficult for her to recognize her own feelings and those of others.
4. *Desire for her mother's love.* Totally repressed, this desire was expressed in desperate bids for attention.

In addition to the psychoanalytic themes, the following external realities also contributed to the formation of Rachel's personality:

1. Mother's early dedication to the teaching profession allowed her to neglect her child while dealing constructively with unconscious guilt over rejective wishes
2. Mother's loss of her nurturant outlet in teaching exacerbated the conflict of wills with Rachel
3. Compensatory external factors:
    a) Availability of devoted nurses
    b) Her special value to the mother as a model child, in serving as proof that the mother had not harmed her excessively by carrying out repressed negative impulses

c) Her scapegoat role, through which the status quo of the marriage was maintained; her consequent importance to both parents as a connecting link between them

d) Lack of real hostility on the part of the mother (indicated by scarcity of markedly destructive incidents)

To protect the developing self during this period of her life, Rachel developed these useful strategies for ego defense (not all are, strictly speaking, classical defenses):

1. *Denial* of loving feelings toward the mother by refusing to be like her.

2. *Passive-aggressive behavior*—by evading their efforts to train and discipline her, she was able to induce her own feeling state in her parents. When they erupted in anger, they experienced the helplessness and lack of control that were normal for her.

3. *Development of a "tough" facade*, to keep the budding self safe from injury; through false bravado and presentation of herself as a "misfit," she protected the precariously formed self from exposure to ridicule and rejection.

4. *Projection* of longing for her parents onto religious institutions or their representatives, which stood in for unassimilated parts of herself.

5. *Belief in magical solutions* to adult problems through mystical experiences; to childhood problems through the wish to eject a bad self incapable of coexisting with a good self (revealed in unintegrated SIS responses).

6. *Intellectualization*, to avoid looking inward; steeping herself in religious doctrine and psychological theories are variants of this defense.

With the exception of intellectualization, Rachel's primitive defense structure and perceptions indicated a very early stage of development that confined her to a highly constricted world in which she and her mother were alone. (This is reflected in the preponderance of dyads in her SIS stories and in her rejection of the partiarchal god image in real life.)

In times of deep insecurity, such as that in which I found her during her first interview when the loss of her mother was still relatively recent, Rachel's defenses enabled her to cope. During that initial session, she clung tenaciously to her old habit of hating mother as a defense against emergent love, even though doing so threatened the symbiosis. It was only after her self-acknowledged psychological rebirth between interviews that Rachel was able to relax her defenses markedly and thereby make a psychological reunion with her mother possible.

The energy she formerly invested in fortifying her defenses expanded into an abundance of good feelings as she worked out the issues raised to consciousness by her vision. But her vision was only the beginning. Indeed her very reluctance to give up these good feelings (as if it meant giving up mother) suggests the absence of a reliable maternal presence in her unconscious. It took years of exploring the labyrinth of the unconscious before Rachel was able to fill this void; even now she sometimes resurrects her mother by latching on to men in whom she detects maternal aspects. Thinly disguised oedipal stories suggest that she wanted mother in the most primal sense all along.

Nevertheless, once the initial burst of happiness that accompanied her vision wore off and she came back to earth, Rachel was able to recognize hard truths about both her parents and herself and, as a consequence, to become more self-accepting. With a more substantial self to rely on, Rachel was less vulnerable and needy, more able to make the peace with her mother that her own psychological freedom demanded.

Moving Forward

Knowing how hard old habits—like hating a mother—are to break, I could never have anticipated the genuine awe and admiration I would note in Rachel's voice when, at her second interview, she described her mother's valiant ten-year battle with cancer. By then, the bitterness she had always felt toward her mother was gone, a sincere respect for the way the older woman had managed her dying having led Rachel to reassess her mother's life and death.

By the time we met for the second interview, a year and a half after the first one, I could see in a moment that Rachel was different. Her appearance had changed, apparently from the inside out. She seemed happier, more comfortable inside her own skin, more free to be herself. Certain behaviors noted in the first interview were still in evidence: the strident voice, the inappropriate affect, the tendency to interrupt. They seemed, however, to be under greater control, and she no longer seemed to focus on herself as the center of the universe.

Not unaware of these changes in herself, Rachel was exhilarated by newly discovered growth possibilities. She spoke of her ongoing quest for meaning and wholeness in her life but was also eager to share the occasional, luminous moments that now punctuated long stretches of uncertainty. The brightest of the bright lights was a wonderful dream, about which she said with an altogether new sense of pride, "I deserved that dream." It was so good that it seemed like a gift, a reward for superb accomplishments. In a way, that is what it was.

She described the manifest content of the dream in these words: "A voice told me I would be taught about the process of aging. Then a black and white diagram appears, representing an aspect of God to which we can relate, since no one can understand God completely. Out of a half-moon shape emerge two cheerful-looking godheads. Underneath this configuration but also connected to the godheads is the head of an earthy old man."

Rachel recalled her dream-self as being fascinated with the pair of godheads (which she saw as representing male and female aspects of herself) as if, reluctant even during the dream itself to deal with her own aging, she was tempted to distract herself from the dream's thematic content by dwelling on this interesting pair. But she was not to be distracted: "The voice explained the positive aspects of the aging process, namely, that as we grow older, God becomes younger; when we die, God is reborn; and when we are born, God is old. So if old people are looked upon by young people as childish, it has to do with the process of rejuvenation of the godhead."

The associations Rachel attached to her creative fantasy suggest an unconscious attempt to merge the two Rachels, one, the "eternal girl" described by Jung, and the other, the knowledgeable and wise adult she has been striving to become. She understood the imperative transmitted by her "voice" as a warning not to lose "the inner child," the potential we are born with. Losing it, "we lose our connection to the divine." And with it, we lose the possibility of a fulfilling old age.

Rachel's concern about losing her "child" in this description of her dream echoes her description of the boat scene (similar to figure 5), where the "little boat" (or little woman) "is forgotten—will rot." The fear of self-loss is intimately tied to mother loss, understandably, since without the mother the child will die. But Rachel's concern, which is surely linked with the loss of her mother, is assuaged by the dream voice, which, like the serenity of the boat scene, comforts her. She feels good about the message through which her dream voice—and, therefore, she herself—makes positive assertions about growing older. She confirms internally the observation of Erik Erikson that aging need not be perceived as synonymous with depletion and loss but can instead be a consolidation of life's stages, bringing an altogether new sense of wholeness and purposes achieved.[7] Such a positive feeling state, often linked with recaptured memories of closeness to one's mother or mother surrogate, was what psychoanalyst-pediatrician D.W. Winnicott described as the "capacity to be alone" that is, the ability to function independently on the basis of a reservoir of caring accrued in the past.[8]

Rachel, more consciously than most, had long sought to achieve this sense of wholeness through a connection with the divine. Her determined spiritual quest brought her little reward. I take her observation that older people are "often religiously affiliated but only rarely connected" as a generalization of her own particular inability to find inner peace through religious channels.

She certanly knew what she was looking for. She had earlier projected her desire for such fulfillment onto the boat (pictured on card 5), which she saw as retired from transporting "joyful little children down the river" of life. Now serenely merged into "part of the whole scene," the boat that Rachel describes reflects a childlike belief in the omnipotent fusion of symbiosis. At the time she devised the story containing this affirmative view of aging, she held to a duel view of old age, reflecting the split within herself (so that, for all the serenity of the scene, she notes that the boat will surely rot). By the time that she experienced the aging dream, the division was beginning to narrow.

The dream itself was a dynamic part of the resolution process, revealing many facets of Rachel's internal complexity. It manages to integrate a young and an older version of herself (the dual view again) in an attempt to restore balance and continuity to the whole self through a harmonious familial triad in which the father, as the fount of worldly knowledge, "leads the child out into the world."[9] Taken as a whole, the theme of Rachel's aging dream is self-expansion. Moving beyond her earlier efforts to transcend her personal limitations—through leaps of faith or magical visions—the dream reveals her understanding of the psychological processes that will make her whole. The dream enhances the dreamer because it crystallizes the working-through process and leaves her a different, more complicated, and enriched person.

Moveover, although it is focused on aging and death, the dream represents a tribute to life that is made possible when Rachel became ready, at last, to surrender long-cherished illusions about herself, and about her parents as well, as can be seen, to give one example, in the elevation of her father to Olympian heights. (Notice how ungodlike the worldly father figure appears in the dream.) Once she was able to view herself more realistically and more generously, she no longer needed the romantic illusions she had created around the memories of her parents. It is believed that such reevaluation comes from learning in treatment that the therapist is human and fallible and, therefore, living proof that one does not have to be perfect to be loved, that it is quite simply OK to be imperfect.

Rachel's unconscious deliberations through this dream set her on the path to greater maturity and provided her with a helpful blueprint for growth. The dream helped her to recognize and appreciate her psychological development during a transitional stage. That Rachel has yet to complete the integrative work diagrammed in the dream cannot come as a surprise to anyone who recognizes the difficulties inherent in the psychoanalytic process, a process that Girard Franklin characterized as a long, often arduous "adventure into the unknown, and possibly unknowable."[10]

Rachel, the adventuresome one, welcomes the continuing challenge.

Notes

1. Bruno Bettelheim, quoted in Marie Cardin, *The Words to Say It* (Cambridge: Van Vactor and Goodheart, 1983), 308.
2. Otto Kernberg, quoted in Margaret S. Mahler and Louise Kaplan, "Developmental Aspects in the Assessment of Narcissistic and So-called Borderline Personalities," in *Borderline Personality Disorders*, ed. Peter Hartocollis (New York: International Universities Press, 1977), 77.
3. Roy R. Grinker, Sr., "The Borderline Syndrome: A Phenomenological View," in *Borderline Personality Disorders*, ed. Peter Hartocollis (New York: International Universities Press, 1977), 167.
4. J.G. Gunderson and M. Singer, "Defining Borderline Patients: An Overview," *American Journal of Psychiatry* 132(1975):1-10.
5. Otto F. Kernberg, "Borderline Personality Organization," *Journal of the American Psychoanalytic Association* 15(1967):641-85.
6. Grinker, "The Borderline Syndrome," 159-72.
7. Erik H. Erikson, *Childhood and Society* (New York: W.W. Norton, 1963), 268.
8. D.W. Winnicott, *The Maturational Process and the Facilitating Environment* (New York: International Universities Press, 1965), 29-36.
9. Ernest L. Abelin, "The Role of the Father in the Separation-Individuation Process," in *Separation-Individuation*, ed. Margaret S. Mahler (New York: International Universities Press, 1971), 229-50.
10. Girard Franklin, "The Quest for Certainty in Psychoanalytic Therapy," in *Psychologist-Psychoanalyst* 6, no. 1 (1985), 4.

9
Separate but Together

I guess I am just good at relationships," Paula told the interviewer at their first session. It was astute of her to recognize what may well have been the secret to her happiness in her later life. Although her mother had died many years before, Paula was able to call on loving feelings for her even after her only child died of pneumonia. Paula was able to regain her balance quickly after her tragic loss, using her misfortune to bring her closer to other people in her life. She remained as generous and empathetic as she had always been.

The source of Paula's good feelings lay deep in her earliest relationships. She described a particularly warm and loving mother-daughter relationship in which she was early appreciated as a distinct and worthwhile person. In this and in other respects, she is typical of the most mature group of women studied, all of whom reflect a firm sense of self and greater than normal capacity for developing close relationships.

Overall high functioning scores eleven years after her mother's death showed Paula to be fully recovered from the mourning process. She is "separated" psychologically and chronologically. Like the other subjects who functioned at the highest levels, she is bright, sophisticated, and self-aware. Some of the eight women in this group had worked professionally before retiring; others had participated actively in volunteer work. Most were able to enjoy the special flavor of later life. Even a subject who disparaged her activities as "dilettantish" was nonetheless able to find much of the same pleasure in living that had enriched her younger years. Without exception, these women valued their personal accomplishments less than they did their interpersonal relationships. This was the most consistent characteristic of this population.

Early childhood experiences were influential in a clearly observable fashion. Nearly half of these women reported childhood memories of being treated as "important though little" or "special" by their fathers as well as by their mothers. The internalization of this environmental factor was demonstrated in the significant correlation between the degrees of separation and of outcome functioning shown by the test results.

The members of this group of mature and separated women are both nurturing and competent in the community as well. These women find no conflict in taking on different roles at the same time. One subject described teaching and raising a family as "mutually rewarding pursuits," thereby expressing a sentiment common to the members of the group. Their high levels of both internal and external functioning are clear indexes of how well they have learned to integrate the various aspects of their individual selves.

The traditional mother role did not impede the development of unique and separate identities for these women, and that it held a priority position in their value systems seems to have set the stage for other accomplishments. The crucial variable, in terms of predicting functioning, turned out to be acceptance of personal dependency. And the greater the subject's self-acceptance (growing out of optimal mothering given her as an infant), the greater is her current ability to interact with others in an interdependent way.

In short, optimally functioning women found that loving relationships with others were crucial to a full, rich life. They were able to affirm their need for others without feeling in any way diminished by that need, confirming in their lives the idea that personal maturity does not require total independence from other persons.

Psychoanalytic theorists, in fact, include the need for others in the most sophisticated stages of development. The mature women were able to experience intimacy (in Erickson's view, the capacity for loving without losing one's self in another[1]) and were also capable of tolerating enforced solitude in their lives. In other words, they acted out Winnicott's idea of a mature "capacity to be alone"[2] (which is based on the implied memory that someone, usually the mother, was once there) by being able to love without "getting lost" in another at the same time. This paradoxical state of being both inside and outside a relationship (known as dual unity) originates in the child's experience within the symbiotic orbit, in which the child has the illusion of being one with the mother. Our everlasting longing for this absolutely protected state is juxtaposed to the need to adjust to an essentially hostile world; this explains why separation is as difficult as it is. Even for the most mature individuals, there is no such thing as smooth sailing on the seas of separation.

Complex emotional forces drive us all to stay connected to others.[3] When significant others are not available, the need for connectedness is often played out on a spiritual level. We saw this poignantly expressed in Rachel's "aging dream" in which she sought spiritual connection to the divine through her inner child. Like her, some of the healthiest subjects in the study also turned to religion when their personal relationships began to dwindle. I might add that I consider it no accident that Rachel, and other, more mature women, found eventual fulfillment of their spiritual quests in Judaism; this religion combines the belief in one god—mirroring one's own wholeness—with the meeting of dependency needs, an echo of the paradox of being alone with someone. I do not mean to suggest that other monotheistic faiths do not also have spiritually whole people among their adherents. It so happens that these women were exposed to Judaism and found it responsive to their needs.

Feelings of maternal closeness can be expanded to include communion with nature as well as religious experiences. Almost all the women in this group projected the same sense of serene fulfillment onto the boat picture (resembling figure 5), which seemed to have a special meaning for them. Their stories were consistent, the quality of affect invariably pleasant, as in Marie's "very quiet pond and quiet forest . . . nice time of year, serene feeling."

Moreover, the experience for the subjects of relating stories to a nature scene proved to be an integrative one that struck a resonant chord in my own personal history. I remember feeling a sense of completeness as a child whenever I roamed through the family garden by myself. My analyst, on hearing of my recollection, attributed my happiness in that setting to the fact that I was not alone, but "with Mother Nature." Spoken half in jest, the comment led me to realize that it is partly because the wonders of nature do provide comfort in times of loneliness and stress that people have come to mythologize nature in maternal terms and symbols.

I originally expected responses to the unstructured boat scene to be revealing about separation issues—for example how distinctly one sees one's self in relation to the world. Instead, the scene stimulated positive feelings related to reunion with loved ones after death or the acceptance of personal limitations; the boat's passage was generally equated with the awesome journey of life as if the women unconsciously were aware of Erikson's observation that the mature person may, in the final stage in the life cycle, come to view death as the termination of a meaningful trip.[4]

The commonality of this theme brought out, quite unexpectedly, something useful about later life issues. The need to bring closure and consistency to one's life overrules other considerations when older women see this scene in card 5. In fact, the mere presentation of this card ensured a harmonious end to the interview procedure; the subject's story alone seemed to enhance her.

These women seemed to be saying that love is what has given meaning to their lives. Nothing is more important to the harmony that marks their mature years than the glow (or the afterglow) of their love relationships. This is precisely what is meant by reexperiencing early closeness to the mother. But while they may believe that life is empty without love, these women did not turn their backs on the value of achievement. Still doers and achievers, they are able to creatively impart to others a lifetime of wisdom. An exceptionally devoted teacher, and a "retired" social worker who leads senior citizens in lively political discussions, are two impressive examples. Without exception, they were able to strike the balance between love and work that Sigmund Freud described as fundamentally important to a psychologically healthy life.

The lives of the group of mature women exemplify the ideal ending for the universal striving for wholeness. Originating in the symbiotic self, their stories are loving expressions of their own symbolic voyages of return to their mothers. Their current sense of self-satisfaction is the enviable reward for becoming at last both separate and together.

Notes

1. Erik H. Erikson, *Childhood and Society* (New York: W.W. Norton, 1963), 263–266.
2. D.W. Winnicott, *The Maturational Process and the Facilitating Environment* (New York: International Universities Press, 1965), 34.
3. Helen Block Lewis, "Psychoanalysis as Therapy Today," *Psychologist-Psychoanalyst* 6, no. 4 (1985–86):12.
4. Erikson, *Childhood and Society*, 269.

10
The Light at the End of the Tunnel

Psychotherapists, who are vulnerable to the same frailties and vanities as other human beings, find great pleasure in witnessing the growth of self-understanding in their clients/patients. It is a pleasure that cannot be summoned at will, there being no power intrinsic to the craft by which even the most skilled therapist can control the cognitive processes, the decisions, or the attitudes of her patient. The ultimate, decisive power to resolve the patient's conflicts resides in the patient, not the therapist, and whatever happens that is good in the psychotherapeutic encounter happens when the patient, with or without help, discovers (or uncovers) a consciousness-altering insight.

Such insights seem to come swiftly and often unexpectedly, despite the usually arduous and probably painful process that has come before. Like mining for gems buried in the earth, the task of finding and bringing to light the unresolved fears and conflicts hidden in the unconscious requires diligence and concentrated effort. The psychotherapeutic process moves the patient toward the treasured insights by promoting a level of confidence in the self and in the therapist that permits a gradual relaxation of the patient's defenses. This relaxation is inevitably hampered by the anxieties of every patient's inner child, which holds on to its childhood fears, refusing to let them go (wishing through its refusal to protect its vital connections with its significant others), no matter how much those fears interfere with adult functioning. As long as these anxieties prevail, the patient cannot accept the truth of insightful interpretations offered by the therapist.

The therapist, through skill and experience, leads patients to freedom from their old childhood fears. Practitioners of psychoanalytic therapy attempt to do this by leading the patient gently back in thought to childhood, where the fears and early perceptions are confronted and reinterpreted. To illustrate this strategy, Winnicott describes a patient who had a very difficult time trusting both himself and the therapist. Winnicott attributed this lack of trust to the patient's "false self," which, unlike the very common false but socially adaptive personae most people adopt as personality masks, threatened in this case to take over the entire personality.[1] Such extreme cases are usually linked to an early lack of rapport between mother and child, but the goal is to have the patient, or the "false" self, entrust the "true self" or child, whom the patient has been shielding, to the caretaker/therapist.

Through repeated encounters with this inner child in the presence of the concerned therapist (who takes on aspects of parental figures), the patient comes to know that certain early fears no longer apply to reality. She comes to see that the parents she once perceived as big and powerful can no longer hurt her, that they cannot retaliate for her "bad thoughts" and that her anger did not kill them (by making them magically disappear). Nor is she, as she believed, at the mercy of impulses that are out of her control.

Eventually, the patient may come to realize that her current fears of abandonment through loss of parental love are unwarranted extensions of childhood distortions. Although such fears may seem foolish when evaluated from the adult perspective, intellectual reasoning will not extinguish them. The patient's adult thought processes alone are insufficient for accomplishing that task; the inner child must go back to the time in the patient's life when such fears were very real and well grounded, and confront them.

What happens in psychoanalytic treatment is that the patient's child learns to trust the therapist in a way that's different from the adult perception of the same relationship. The residual child comes to experience the therapist as a consistent and caring parent who knows and understands the deepest anxiety that is being experienced. Although showing this understanding usually takes the form of communicating verbally at the appropriate moment, there are times when words of comfort and consolation from the therapist are of little use. It is the therapist's being "in tune" with or believing in the reality of the patient's primitive anxiety (a fear of disintegrating, or of falling forever, in the case of some very disturbed patients) that makes the patient able to endure the pain of regression to a dependent state.

The adult patient, for whom dependency is highly distressing (it seems nonadult) and risky (will the therapist "be there"?), draws solace from the therapist's comforting presence. This emotional equivalent of a mother's holding her child, which Winnicott aptly calls "holding the patient,"[2] allows the patient to dare to explore the recesses of her unconscious, just as the child she once was could venture out into the real world when she was filled up with mothering. This new way of taking part in a relationship must be experienced over and over again before it becomes part of the total person, until the most primitive part of her is utterly convinced that she will not be forsaken for expressing her whole self. The empathy and understanding of the therapist over a period of time help bring the patient to make lasting changes.

Marie's Progress

It was this type of experience in therapy that eventually helped Marie to confront her problems. She needed to trust herself enough to regress to an infantile state if she was to improve. However, this did not mean going back to being a child again, contrary to the common misperception about therapy. An adult can never do that because of the vast experience she has accumulated. The process is complicated; the patient/nursemaid brings his child to be treated, and the therapist sometimes must address all these people at once!

But the therapist is not the parent, any more than the patient is the child she once was or still wishes to be. Rather, the patient has an opportunity to grow up better through psychotherapy. And indeed regression may be altogether essential for "false," compliant types like Marie, if this process is to occur.

Although it is true that one can never reexperience one's childhood, Marie sometimes needed to repair ruptures associated with preverbal experiences that she had endured alone. She had responded to the rebuffs from her parents (who had persuaded her that she was less than perfect and therefore unlovable) by developing a false, compliant personality sustained by behaviors that would cause no offense to her parents. An individual whose life is structured on such a rationale begins to feel unreal to herself and to manifest brittle, shallow personality traits.

Marie thus came to therapy feeling that life was a cruel joke in which her best efforts were rewarded with impoverishment, both financial and spiritual. Her spoken emphasis was on the monetary deprivations she was suffering, but her symbolic complaint was one of disappointment at the disappearance of the once bountiful maternal breast; there was no mothering to soothe the pains of her old age.

Before Marie could accept this truth about her ancient but current need for mothering, she had to learn more about herself as her father's daughter. Her account suggests that her relationship with her father was particularly close, excluding for their own purposes a mutually belittled mother. Even before father and daughter became collaborators in business ventures, Marie had been a doer and an achiever. She had resolved the problem of oedipal rivalry with her mother by defining herself as her father's favorite "son." Pursuant to a theory developed by Gutmann, this self-definition permitted her to join her father "through the fleshless intellect, rather than through the senses."[3]

To maintain her connection with him (and later with her husband, with whom she had the same sort of spiritual partnership), Marie joined her father in disparaging her mother and women in general as weak and ineffectual creatures. It followed logically that she would not give herself to motherhood, whose challenges could not be as personally gratifying to her as the possibilities offered by the then typically male business world.

Progress in therapy is never linear. There are ups and downs and roundabouts. Early in therapy, Marie would have totally rejected the construction of her relationships just offered. She did not see herself as disparaging her mother at all; it was her mother who rejected *her*, who gave her the reason to go off "innocently" with her father, more in self-defense than in anger. Furthermore, as far as Marie was concerned, putting down women had nothing whatsoever to do with her feelings about her own mother, whom she "worshipped."

By her own account, Marie was never happier than during the glory days of collaboration with father. She felt totally in control of her life and gave no thought to what might come next. Believing that what she did not know could not hurt her, she blocked the memory of her childhood sadness. It was only during the chipping-away process of her therapy that her vested interest in denial became clear to her, that she came to realize that the less mature part of her had believed she could avoid pain, as she once put it, "if I just kept my eyes closed."

Success in the business world had concentrated her focus outside herself and had provided her with some rewards. Her competence in this arena allowed her to demonstrate her ability to live and operate at a safe distance from the mother who threatened to engulf her. She was thus able to create a psychological island on which her ego could develop and grow, without constant intrusion by her mother. While Rachel was able to accomplish something like this by indirect efforts, Marie's definition and tireless pursuit of this self-enhancing objective made her achievement a qualitatively different one.

Her successes did not, however, put an end to her retaliatory wishes, in which she wanted to "abolish" both her mother and her sister (to whom she had lost her pivotal position in the family); these hidden objectives were disguised as global anxiety and concern over her husband's health. Marie was starting to get in touch with these feelings when her treatment ended.

She had at one time imagined that she could live out her father's dreams better than a real son could. Her subsequent growth could not protect her from the damaging narcissistic wounds that she had sustained when she was most vulnerable. In the slow, painful uncovering process in which "holding" played a part, Marie repeatedly came face-to-face with the most primitive part of herself that still feels helpless. Working through these feelings helped her become more empathetic to her whole self.

A look on the theoretical level at Marie's history shows an infantilizing mother who prolonged the symbiotic subphase, thereby endangering the positive contributions of subsequent phases of Marie's development. Deprived of the two principal sources of healthy narcissism, the narcissistic enhancement from within (which accrues from the autonomous achievements of practicing) and the external enhancement (which comes from the environment), Marie apparently could not bask in the warm glow of what Mahler and Kaplan describe as "libidinally mirroring friendly adults"[4] and to which, in my view, every child has a rightful claim. It was her misfortune to be treated as a narcissistic extension by both of her parents.

Her compensatory sense of grandiosity collapsed well beyond the normal rapprochement phase, when narcissism and, particularly, omnipotence are known to be especially vulnerable to an insufficient buildup of reserves. Nevertheless, the distortion of one subphase[5] should not obscure the fact that corrective influences from other phases, and well beyond, can undo some of the damage. That is why Marie is now as healthy as she is, despite the lingering vulnerability from the rapprochement crisis, which cast a shadow on all subsequent development. Marie's record of achievement, which she shared with the healthiest women in the study, was an important source of self-esteem, and it thereby helped her offset a serious developmental imbalance. That she was able to function productively throughout most of her life without psychiatric intervention supports this observation.

After being in treatment for about a year, Marie was able to describe a pictured gymnast climbing a rope as "smiling and performing well." Viewing herself so positively suggests considerable ego strength on Marie's part. That she saw herself capable of continuing growth and achievement was apparent in her very first story (in relation to card 2; figure 2), in which she announced, "I'm going to make something much better of myself." (This fragment demonstrates the test's ability to evoke the essence of the whole person in one statement.) Marie has at this point in her life moved quite a long way toward gaining her ambitious objective.

What part therapy played in her progress is hard to assess in precise, scientific terms, but the therapeutic encounter was certainly informative about the patient. Marie's noisy demands for special treatment—for reduced fees, for isolated treatment rooms—suggested the possibility that her mother did not gratify her need for exclusive attention after her sister was born. Perhaps the mother first extricated herself from an uncomfortable situation by angrily pushing Marie away—or perhaps Marie angrily withdrew first. Test responses (below) suggest that there must have been a long-standing pattern of maternal failure to provide a balance of intermittent body closeness during practicing (when the child returns to mother for periodic refueling), with the effect that Marie was deprived of much needed bodily contact. Her independence may have been bought at the expense of bodily closeness.[6]

Retrospectively, it is clear that Marie's childhood demands for attention declined, not because Marie had resolved her rapprochement crisis, but because she had abandoned hope. The data strongly support this construction. Marie's test results included (1) many "t" or texture responses to the Rorschach, suggesting contact hunger; (2) mostly conventional proper responses oriented toward the world in a highly realistic way to this same test, indicating a denial of more primal needs; (3) efforts on Marie's part to free herself from entanglement noted in SIS stories, suggesting an inability to count on an ego-supportive mother; and (4) demands by Marie for special treatment, perpetuating the fantasy that sibling rivals (my other patients) do not exist.

Marie treated me as a captive audience from whom she anticipated mirroring admiration. She seemed to be trying to recapture the ideal state of self she had experienced in her early years as the queen bee of the nursery. My nonjudgmental explanation of the function of her old narcissistic needs (healthy needs that had not been fulfilled early in life) demonstrated to her that I was in tune with her disintegration anxiety as well as with the protective function of her grandiose fantasies.[7] Because I did not censor their expression, Marie was able to reexperience her longing for her mother's (read "therapist's") wholehearted and joyful acceptance of her early sense of grandiosity in the context of an all-giving surrounding. Although there was some continuing tension between her often voiced demands and my goal of avoiding interference with the spontaneously arising transference mobilization of old needs, treatment proceeded without my yielding to all of Marie's demands. The number of actual interventions was actually limited to one: Marie's fee was reduced to accommodate her financial situation.

Treatment ended for Marie when she and her husband moved to a distant state to live out their retirement years. By that time, her narcissistic grandiosity was giving way to normal assertiveness. She had stopped making demands. Her habit of bringing food into therapy sessions (her own "supplies") had ceased when she discovered the availability of the regular "feedings" she perceived herself to be receiving from treatment. Her sense of increased freedom to be herself was expressed in efforts to broaden her social network. She hired a part-time nurse for her husband so that she could more actively pursue newly discovered interests: she started meeting with persons in similar circumstances (that is, families of invalids), enrolled in a writing course, and joined a theater group. She also "indulged" her growing taste for psychotherapy by seeking further treatment, having given up her need to feel guilty when she did not in fact feel guilty about something.

These self-expansive behaviors suggested that therapy was of subjective benefit to Marie. It had taken many months of treatment to overcome her inner sense of futility. All the success she had achieved in the world as a smoothly functioning performer was attributable to the false self she had developed to protect her true self. Having playacted most of her life, she had been unable to take pleasure in her own achievements. She had seemed phony to herself.

Her friends had not penetrated the false shell. "All my friends were convinced I was making it," she once commented sadly while describing "fifty years of wasted life." It was a tremendous leap for her to start enjoying the daily pleasures of living. Her happiness was as real as her distress had been. It was gratifying for me to see Marie at last feel real and anxious to live life to the fullest.

Rachel's Progress

Rachel, who unlike Marie did not undergo psychoanalytically oriented treatment, is also enjoying happier days. Her therapy was limited to serious introspection based on her studies of psychology and philosophy, supplemented by casual conversations with me. The progress she has been able to make is quite remarkable. Over the relatively short time period that I have known her, and especially since she experienced the aging dream, she has become increasingly more realistic and better centered. Her feelings of euphoria are less extreme now that they come from a quiet inner center; ironically, they stay with her longer. While visions of Luther no longer blind her with brilliance, she is also spared the precipitous plunges into darkness. She seems to have left the emotional brinks for safer middle ground.

In this postdream consolidation period, Rachel is not immune to the failures that are a part of experimenting with previously untried approaches to life. She seems to have developed greater tolerance for ambiguity, a valuable trait for coping with the exigencies of human experience, in the reality of which there can be no perfect resolution of separation issues. In life, total consonance between inner and outer experience exists only in dreams.

Rachel had a chance to test the strength of her revitalized self when her son Michael recently announced his decision to leave the family home and move to a distant state. I happened by chance to telephone her soon after the decision was announced. She was, she confessed to me, distraught over the imminent separation and the (remote) possibility of never seeing her son again. Still, she was reasonably confident that the eventual outcome would be favorable and even acknowledged the likelihood that her son had no other way available to him to establish his independence. "Maybe there was no other way for him to do it," she said.

The very fact that Rachel felt depressed and could share her sadness was an encouraging sign of ego strength. She seemed up to the task of coping with guilt and ambivalence and disruption. I told her so and left her to reassemble the elements of her reality, all the while imagining that she was more shattered than she really was.

My assurances to Rachel were not given without reservations. I kept to myself my skepticism about her ability to weather this crisis, doubts attributable in part to the fact that she had never been a patient, or gone through the conventional integration process in therapy, in part to countertransference (the analyst's experience of emotional attachment to the patient) linked with my personal desire to put closure on her life. Reminding myself that the toddler stumbles many times before mastering the skill of upright locomotion, I hoped for the best.

In a follow-up call a few weeks later, I knew immediately from the sound of Rachel's voice that all was well between her and her son. Their relationship is healthier now that he lives in another state, and she realizes the mistakes she made in overprotecting him from childhood dangers at phase appropriate times. She therefore deprived him of the opportunity to achieve a sense of mastery over his environment, the main source of narcissistic enhancement from within, which is the same opportunity she herself had been denied. Additionally, she admits now to having overestimated her son's creative and intellectual potential so that, as they both agree now, "it was quite a shock for him to discover that he was ordinary."

She is able now to recognize that help and support became available to her when she stopped blaming the world for her misfortunes. I was delighted to hear her say that the interviewing process had helped her, particularly because the statement reflected her new expansiveness. With more to give, she can afford to be generous, which is precisely why there is now greater mutuality and trust, as well as love, between her and Michael.

As gratifying as Rachel's progress is, it was puzzling to me that she could do the developmental work necessary to the resolution of separation issues without the benefit of either professional help or a reciprocal, ongoing love relationship, a category in which the mother-son relationship, so often exploitative until recently, could not belong. I spoke openly about this with her and found that she did not see herself traveling a solitary path.

Rachel instead saw herself in a series of love relationships with God or with persons invested with godlike qualities. These relationships sustained her. When disappointed by life or by herself, she turned to religious readings for solace or catharsis. Comparing herself to Job, who suffered through many trials and travails before "God made himself clear to him, as he did to me," she uses religion in effect the way others use psychotherapy: to come to terms with her own life.

The best understanding of Rachel's route to inner peace can be gained through recourse once more to the useful frame of reference provided by the psychological world of the child. It is an apt analogy since Rachel's adult movement toward complete personhood parallels the developing child's progress on the separation-individuation continuum and illustrates how the problems of separation recur throughout the life cycle. From this perspective, Rachel was able after her mother died to contact the child she once was. In mourning her mother, she was able to overcome the distancing defenses built up over the years by reliving preverbal memories of receiving gratification from the early mother-child relationship. The revival of these loving feelings allowed her to feel "well mothered" so that she could in effect mother herself. Recovering these lost positive feelings is the emotional equivalent of finding her inner child, a prerequisite for becoming a more separate and whole person in her own right.

With this renewed contact with her inner child, Rachel no longer needed to keep her suffocating hold on her flesh-and-blood child. Her ability to separate, though reluctantly, from her son Michael is perhaps the best indication of her progress in resolving separation issues. She was not yet able to behave like the mother birds described by Mahler, which, without the neurotic hang-ups of their human counterparts, are able to shove their offspring gently out of the nest,[8] but she was able to cope in effective fashion with the separation initiated by her son. The next step for her may be getting to know her inner child better.

However, in defiance of his own basic precepts, Freud suggested late in his career that psychological insight may not be a prerequisite for curing emotional disorders (thereby throwing some doubt on the validity of his earlier thinking and some light on the limitations of understanding in the best of us). It was with somewhat limited insight that Rachel "treated" herself; she seemed to understand "ego alien" aspects of others better than she could understand herself. Although her mental acuity sometimes actually created barriers to self-understanding, she relied on her considerable intellectual and creative powers to help her cope with the recurrent depressions through which her problems with separation and loss manifested themselves. Using her analytical ability to create distance, she was able to relegate her problems to an intellectual realm devoid of feeling. A loner, afraid of interpersonal relationships, she created a rich inner world that she was able to call on when her mother died. She used the mourning period for intense and apparently self-healing creativity, manifested in part by vivid, third-person accounts of her sense of loss.

Although her self-help methods were not totally successful and her circuitous route no doubt was more time-consuming than it might have been with the help of a therapist, it is fair to say that Rachel managed to get herself "on the way" (Mahler's term to describe the ultimate movement towards separation). Even were it possible to separate completely, we would not wish this for Rachel, or for anyone else. No one is an island, or outgrows the need to be valued and loved; so "on the way" is just fine.

In any case, it is possible that traditional psychotherapy would not have helped her. Persons like Rachel who are chronically unable to maintain affectionate relations are very likely to be similarly unable to develop a transference in analysis. And without the development of a transference neurosis, the displacement of affect generated by feelings toward the parent onto the therapist, patients are prone to see therapists as *things* to be used. Analysis probably would not have worked successfully for her. Delving into the unconscious is no more than a guessing game in such cases. So it may well be that Rachel's lonely journey into herself was the only one possible for her.

Notwithstanding the perils of that journey, Rachel has reached her goal of becoming more meaningful to herself, a goal closely allied with the psychoanalytic process. It is a positive measure of her determination and solitary persistence that, late in life, she has been able to make significant changes in her self-concept and in her worldview. It is only now that purposefulness has for her replaced meaninglessness and alienation from others.

The Search for Wholeness

Rachel's struggle to achieve wholeness is one with which we can all identify. Having been witness to her despair, we can take pleasure in welcoming the new person brought forth by her own labor (pun intended). Inasmuch as she has come as far as she has, I have reason to be optimistic about Rachel's future and about the potential for change and development in all of us.

In bringing the accounts of these two major subjects to a close, some important similarities and disparities are worth noting. Marie was able, thanks to her excellent endowment, to create a safe distance between herself and her mother, but she paid a heavy price for the achievement: she became estranged from herself. Rachel developed a callous shell to protect herself from harm and also paid a heavy price: she became estranged from the world.

This primary difference was reflected early in the diametrically opposite Rorschach test results of the two women, which led in short order to vastly different treatment goals. Marie's responses to the Rorschach test (on which she had a function score of 13 out of a possible 18 points and a structure score of 23 out of a possible 24) were so proper and so extremely conventional that I wanted to lead her into greater contact with her inner world without causing her to lose her capacity for self-discipline.

With Rachel, the need for control was dominant. Her function score (16 out of 18 points) indicated intellectual liberation, energy, and freedom from constriction, while her critically low structure score (15 out of 24 points) showed her to be near the psychotic border. Again, this showed that Marie was alienated from herself, and Rachel from the world.

Besides the discipline/freedom dimension, the two also differed with respect to male/female orientation and to blame of the self/the world. Each had her own brand of narcissism: the once shallow and superficial Marie, active in social and business arenas, versus the deeper, more introspective Rachel, living in relative social isolation. To become whole, each woman had to develop capacities that the other already possessed.

Both had to work their ways to inner clarity. Marie was able to do much of the work herself, which more typically occurs in the classical analytical setting in which the therapist serves as a "blank screen." At times when she was dealing with preverbal experiences that could not be communicated in the usual manner, listening to her attentively sufficed to convey empathy and understanding, in themselves therapeutic.

At other times, I chose to offer my interpretations, as it is after all the task of the therapist in psychoanalytic treatments to track what is going on internally with the patient. Routinely, I follow her unconscious (or "child") as it makes contact with her conscious mind, in the process allowing my unconscious and hers to meet and interact as part of the treatment. During its course, we develop our own symbolic language. As both participant and observer, I attempt to facilitate the process of self-discovery by timely interventions and interpretations whose analytic content grows with the patient's ever-increasing capacity for looking inward.

With the notable exception, however, of Freud, who analyzed himself, and the less notable exception of persons like Rachel, who must go it alone, most of us need guides to direct us along the course of self-discovery. Having someone along may be the very reason that anyone discovers "The Light at the End of the Tunnel."

Notes

1. D.W. Winnicott, *The Maturational Process and the Facilitating Environment* (New York: International Universities Press, 1965).

2. Ibid., 240.

3. David Gutmann, "The Clinical Psychology of Late Life: Developmental Paradigms" (Presented at the West Virginia Gerontology Conference: Transitions of Aging, Morgantown, W. Va.: May 23–26, 1979).

4. Margaret S. Mahler and Louise Kaplan, "Developmental Aspects in the Assessment of Narcissistic and So-called Borderline Personalities," in *Borderline Personality Disorders*, ed. Peter Hartocollis (New York: International Universities Press, 1977), 73.

5. Ibid., 73.

6. Ibid., 84.

7. Heinz Kohut, "The Disorders of the Self and Their Treatment," *International Journal of Psychoanalysis* 59(1978):413–25.

8. Margaret S. Mahler, *The Psychological Birth of the Human Infant* (New York: Basic Books, 1975), 79.

11
What Does It All Mean?

The completion of the research project I have been describing here may not have brought with it complete illumination of the separation-individuation process (is that ever possible?), but it did bring me to certain conclusions, not the least of which is that there are untold numbers of fascinating women with wonderful stories to tell if anyone bothers to ask. I am glad to have had the opportunity to ask some of them.

Some Conclusions

I am convinced (and more important, they themselves are convinced) that both Marie and Rachel are leading better lives because therapy/self-exploration has helped them become more in touch with their whole selves. While it is unfortunate that their discovery came only when they neared the end of their travels, after years of groping through the darkness, there is little doubt that their remaining days are brighter because of it. With a touch of divine irony, both feel as if their lives are just beginning.

These two women, whose histories we have followed so closely, fought and eventually overcame at least some of the obstacles imposed on them by a culture that fostered dependency in women more than in men and thus made becoming an autonomous person a more protracted process for them. At the opposite end of the spectrum of the study women were the unusual persons to whom the obstacles set in their paths were all but invisible.

I refer to those in the most mature group who had a clear sense of who they were and early on seemed to be wholly at one with their self-images. They achieved the inner freedom to be truly themselves, as well as the outer freedom to conduct their lives in ways best suited to their special needs and talents. This dual achievement represented the spontaneous unfolding of the true self; it was the culmination of all that had gone before.

These top scorers were fortunate in having mothers who adapted unusually well to their needs and expectations over the course of development, and fathers who also played important roles in their identity formation. The middle group of women (that probably means most of us) had to settle for relatively successful maternal adaptation, with "good enough" mothers who acted in ways that did not clash totally with the infantile sense of omnipotence, so that their infants could come to recognize the illusory elements, or the playacting, in their fantasy lives.[1] With greater maturity, they became able to distinguish between fantasy and reality.

This is an important experience for a child, being on the receiving end of the average, good enough mother's willingness to play along with her child's belief in its omnipotence, to the point that she even enjoys the child's delusions vicariously through identification. The resulting feeling of feeling OK and loved allows the child gradually to give up such false beliefs. Consequently, maximal adaptation is not always conducive to learning, which is fortunate for us! (This did not happen to Marie, and explains why she took nearly a lifetime to grow up. When the mother cannot adapt adequately, as in her case, the child is seduced into compliance, into creating a "false self.")

Naturally, most subjects fall in the vast middle ground between the early-to-mature and the just-barely-in-the-nick-of-time variety. Generally speaking, psychosexual development is considered more complex and difficult in women than in men. Girls may be more ambivalently tied to their mothers than boys are, as Mahler believed, in part because of their need to change love objects.[2] One might, therefore, blame the obligatory but paradoxical task of switching allegiance to father while holding onto mother for women's more complex separation and oedipal conflicts.

A useful contribution to the understanding of female psychology came through the work of Dorianne Lebe, whose study of women between the ages of thirty and forty, an age group she believed to be developmentally optimal for the resolution of separation and oedipal issues, produced a new developmental timetable.[3] By her thirties, the average woman has had ample opportunity to observe her mother both as weak and ineffectual and as strong, with the consequence that her early inner object representation of her mother has been modified. She has had time for her own achievements in career, marriage and family, and community affairs. With the resulting growth in self-esteem, the time is ripe for complete detachment from her mother.[4]

Lebe's timetable is contingent upon freedom from any serious traumatic events in childhood. It gives a more accurate representation than past timetables, based on an incomplete understanding of women's development, of when it is that today's young women have opportunities to achieve on these fronts. A developmental table based solely on my study would push maturation still further forward; although I observed many women at Lebe's crossroad, I found few who had reached it as early in life as Lebe suggests. For the generation represented by my study subjects, separation was still a cause for celebration if only achieved in the golden years, allowances having to be made for the infinite variety of life factors that inevitably stand in the way. (Domineering mothers of the sort that barred the way for Rachel and Marie are an easy example, one that is already much documented. Marie, for instance, was barely able to extricate herself from her mother's suffocating envelopment; her brittle personality kept her from seeing her mother as she really was.)

That only the exceptional woman, in my study, could complete separation by midlife reflects the generational differences between the cohort groups used in Lebe's study and in mine. For all but a few, the era in which the older women in my study lived out the early stages of their lives precluded consideration of personal achievements much before parental responsibilities were over and done with. With prevailing social norms supporting their private perceptions of personal limitation, many of these women were denied, or they denied themselves, the kinds of extrafamilial successes that younger women today take for granted, in the process extending the period of incubation required to build the sense of self-worth requisite for separation.

In this and in other respects, Lebe's study actually meshes with mine. Her findings show women's failing to resolve their oedipal conflicts and entering adulthood only partially separated from their mothers despite their expanded opportunities in the modern world. Like infinite numbers of women before them, they tend to remain dependent on the power and support afforded by their fathers or male partners in a way that inhibits their own creative expression and competence. In continually borrowing strength from men despite her own impressive achievements, Marie is a perfect example of this generation-spanning phenomenon. Indeed, she might have gone on being a "little girl" all her life had it not been for the threatened loss of her husband.

These overlapping studies concur in showing that the self-enhancement provided by active doing and achieving fosters growth, as does mothering one's own child. It is indeed reassuring to find such consistency and continuity, particularly when results run counter to psychoanalytically based theory, as they do in this case. Although a bias still exists within the field of psychology toward viewing motherhood as essential to normal, healthy development in women, the new findings indicate that the additional sources of self-esteem now generally available provide the extra distance a woman requires to evaluate her mother realistically. Also, her more differentiated self-view gives the new woman enough confidence that the true self can emerge without fear of loss of love, thereby refuting an earlier biased view within the field, namely, that all women remain infantile throughout their lives. This historical bias perhaps derived from the shorter female life expectancy in Freud's day—when relatively few women could statistically be expected to survive the age of menopause—as well as from the myriad of infantilizing cultural forces to which the women of Freud's time and culture were subject.

Lebe's conclusion that women need extra time to grow and develop is reinforced by my finding that the mature older woman is insulated by her own self-esteem from being crushed by personal losses, including that of her offspring when they grow up and leave home, and that of her parents when they die. Narcissism helps to cushion the later blows just as it helped the child withstand falls from grace at the rapprochement stage. This is the significant correlation the findings showed between separation and functioning, indicating that more separated women generally adapt better to later losses.

Findings Related to Mother- and Daughterhood

Some of the study findings ran counter to expectations. Women in the distant loss group did, as predicted, function better than did the women in the recent loss group in terms of adapting to the losses of their mothers. And women in the distant loss group *were* more separated than were members of the recent loss group—that is, separation was significantly related to outcome functioning. But no significant interaction was found between the recentness of maternal loss and the degree of separation.

The unpredicted lack of interaction may be attributable in part to the small sample size, to the fact that the data were simply not numerous enough to show the association. Or it may be that the assessments were made too early, before the narcissistic women had exhausted their available "supplies" (including spouses, children, grandchildren, and others who filled the void within, and therefore, could ease the pain of old age). Had the evaluations been performed five or ten years later, these superficially well-functioning women might have performed less impressively.

As it was, as long as others were around to prop them up, these bright and competent narcissistic women were able to use their intellects to compensate for their shrinking selves—selves in danger of "disappearing" because, like Marie's false self, they had been built on shaky ground. For this reason, cognitive endowment was more closely related to outcome functioning than separation was. Poor performances on the Rorschach measure of internal functioning suggest that these women were indeed on a downward emotional slope.

To the fundamental question of whether the mothering experience per se has consequences for a woman's mental health, there was no clear and definitive answer. In my group of study women, no one pattern assured happiness or psychological well-being in old age. Some of the women were able to use motherhood optimally for their own growth while others were not, the outcome apparently being heavily contingent upon the quality of the mothering originally experienced by the women themselves. Because the value of reaching developmental milestones like parenthood can be undone by the residual effect of early deficits, the study findings suggest that psychological well-being in later life hinges less on parental status than on development of a full and unique personality, the result of having been "well mothered" to begin with.

So it is not possible to say to young women contemplating having children that motherhood is the exclusive route to maturity. Surely what maturity this experience brings is more a welcome result than a premeditated goal of the process. No scientific examination of the lives of the most successful study women can, in any case, distinguish the precise childhood factors from the experiences of parenthood that contributed to those women's ultimate personal successes (excepting only a longitudinal study in which changes in the same individuals are studied over the entire span of development), so we can safely draw only some general conclusions from this preliminary investigation.

Clearly, there is more than one way to grow up. Motherhood turns out to be one way for some women, who are strengthened by it in meeting life's vissicitudes. The most successful women in the study, resourceful at combining child rearing with other pursuits, gave evidence to the belief that a woman's self-esteem is best served by developing both the maternal and the achieving side of herself.

This is precisely the study's most firmly established finding: life is best for maternal, sensitive women who value feelings and relationships but who also manage to acquire personal nondomestic competencies. Motherhood made some women feel good about themselves. For others, the experience only heightened their anxiety and increased their sense of worthlessness or inferiority. Without exception, the early mother-child relationship was very important. It seems, on reflection, that the essence of maternity surpasses the fact of maternity as a factor in personal growth. Toward that goal, being maternal is evidently more important than being a mother.

Being maternal, which entails acceptance of one's own dependency longings, is a quality that profoundly affects later adjustment, whether it comes into play in mother-child interactions or in other intimate relationships, though it is possible that other close relationships outside the mother-child sphere can be similarly conducive to growth opportunities.

Such relationships, including some with surrogate mothers (and in addition to spouses, aunts, or older sisters, therapists may fulfill a parenting function in the broad sense), provided important compensations in the lives of several of the diverse women in my study, who ranged from an anguished mother who had lost her much-loved only child to a struggling single mother of thirteen children whom she devoutly aspired to keep out of jail.[5]

Now that an ever-increasing number of women with and without children work at challenging jobs outside the home, the finding that personal achievement is essential to maturation is, while not startling in its novelty, a conclusion with far-reaching implications. For if the findings of this study are correct (or if replication increases our confidence in them), it may be that the woman who works outside the home is doing something positive for her mental health, irrespective of her own parental status, and that her mental health requires a solid relational balance in her life, whether or not she works outside the home.

While responsive to the changes in women's lives, these new findings also reaffirm more traditional social values. Young women who have made or are still considering making commitments to family, career, or a combination of both might benefit from the experiences of those who walked similar paths before them. What these older women knew so well was that being motherly enriches one throughout life by increasing one's loving capacity.

So if we wish to increase our knowledge of ourselves, let us expand our attention to what other societies have known instinctively, that the old have much to teach us. Increased understanding of the dynamics of aging may make value reassessment and life decisions easier for legions ambivalent women. This small study, based on the current and retrospective examination of the lives of thirty-nine women, may be a step toward increasing that understanding.

Beyond Separation

This study has raised many socially relevant questions that would be worth exploring. To do a comparative study of separation in childless women and in mothers would be the logical next step. For example, do childless women suffer from something akin to postpartum depression in old age, like some immature mothers? That merely procreating does not ensure growth is exemplified by the case of Marie, who, despite her motherhood and noteworthy achievements, failed to develop the loving side of herself. Work became a means of escaping from the escalating demands of her needy infant, who was a painful reminder of her own vulnerability. In that, she resembles some modern career women I have observed.

So we can already say on the basis of the present study that problems in later life have more to do with a generally disturbed childhood than with being or not being a parent, since the difficulties of the subjects in the study were often in evidence before their childbearing years. In fact, Rachel and others had operated on the thin edge from childhood onward. We know too the importance that good mothering plays from the moment of birth and throughout life. And we know the tenacity with which those who did not get enough of it in childhood continue to seek it—sadly sometimes even from inanimate objects, like the study mother who proudly showed me the doll collection she keeps on her bed—some from supportive spouses, some from their children, some from therapy—until they are finally ready to let go.

We know that some people never recognize their own continuing need for mothering. And we know that some people are simply never ready to let go.

Perhaps future research will tell us why.

Notes

1. D.W. Winnicott, *The Maturational Process and the Facilitating Environment* (New York: International Universities Press, 1965), 57.

2. Margaret S. Mahler, *The Psychological Birth of the Human Infant* (New York: Basic Books, 1975), 106.

3. Dorianne Lebe, "Women and Individuation," *Psychoanalytic Review* 69, no. 1 (1982), 63–73.

4. Ibid. Note that separation occurs when the woman achieves positive identification with her mother. This coincides with acceptance of her femininity, thereby resolving the oedipus complex. What happens is that the young woman discovers that she is not a threat to men and that she may even compete actively with them since she herself does not want to be a man.

5. As noted earlier, these kinds of circumstances did not influence my results. However, there is clearly a vast difference between the wrenching experience of a child's death (at any age) and losing children through the natural processes of growing up, which we need to learn more about—for example, how do these various experiences affect the mother's growth potential? See discussion in Jane B. Abramson, *Evaluation of the Effects of Separation on Adaptation to Loss in Older Women Who Have Lost Their Mothers* (Ann Arbor, Mich.: University Microfilms International, 1985), 105.

Appendix
Description of Testing Instruments and Procedures

Testing Instruments and Procedures

The Testing Instruments

Supplementary information regarding the testing instruments on which I relied for the purposes of the study and in the creation of the SIS scale is provided here.

The Katz Adjustment Scale

In 1963, Martin Katz developed a set of inventories to facilitate objective evaluation of the behavior of psychiatric patients before and after treatment (see the bibliography). His scales are notable for their dual reliance on assessments of social behavior by the patients themselves and by members of their families. Those parts of the symptom checklist (table A-1) that measured adaptation to loss became one of the three outcome indexes used to establish overall functioning of the subjects in this study.

The Harrow Functioning Interview

First developed as part of a study of hospitalized patients, the Harrow interview (see bibliography) offers a number of indexes of mental status, of which these three were relevant to the present research:

1. An index of social adjustment, which combines questions pertaining to social behavior, interpersonal contact, and involvement in activities outside of the home; the patient's first measured level of functioning is used as the baseline
2. An index of occupational adjustment, which measures both objective and subjective aspects of a subject's work performance
3. A subjective evaluation of the subject's mental health

Table A–1
Symptom Checklist

Name: _____ Date: _____

Please answer the following with respect to your personal experiences:

A.

| | *Today or During the Past Few Weeks* | | | |
| | 1 | 2 | 3 | 4 |
	Have not had this complaint	*Bothers me a little*	*Bothers me quite a bit*	*Bothers me almost all the time*
1. Headaches	☐	☐	☐	☐
2. Pains in the heart or chest	☐	☐	☐	☐
3. Heart pounding or racing	☐	☐	☐	☐
4. Trouble getting your breath	☐	☐	☐	☐
5. Faintness or dizziness	☐	☐	☐	☐
6. Difficulty in falling asleep or staying asleep	☐	☐	☐	☐
7. Bad dreams	☐	☐	☐	☐
8. Blaming yourself for things you did or failed to do	☐	☐	☐	☐
9. Feeling generally worried or fretful	☐	☐	☐	☐
10. Feeling blue	☐	☐	☐	☐
11. Being easily moved to tears	☐	☐	☐	☐
12. Feeling you were not functioning as well as you could, feeling blocked or unable to get things done	☐	☐	☐	☐
13. Getting tired easily	☐	☐	☐	☐
14. Feeling keyed up and jittery	☐	☐	☐	☐
15. Having no interest in things	☐	☐	☐	☐
16. Having trouble keeping your mind on what you were doing	☐	☐	☐	☐
17. Loss of appetite	☐	☐	☐	☐

B.

1. Have you been feeling sad or blue over the past few months?
    _____ 1. No, not at all
    _____ 2. A little bit
    _____ 3. A moderate amount
    _____ 4. Quite a bit

2. Have you been depressed over the last few months?
    _____ 1. Quite a bit
    _____ 2. A moderate amount
    _____ 3. A little bit
    _____ 4. No, not at all

Source: Adapted from the Katz scale, in M. Katz, "Methods for Measuring Adjustment and Social Behavior in the Community," *Psychological Reports Monographs* 13(1966):503–35.

Revisions were made to the original Harrow interview to respond to the special features of an older population. A psychotic scale inapplicable to the subjects was eliminated, while references to experiences of mature life, such as grandparenting, which would not have been applicable to the original, younger population, were incorporated. Additionally, the frame of reference was changed from the original "prehospitalization" phase to the period "prior to significant losses."

Responses to questions regarding external functioning were graded numerically and the resulting scores used for placement of the subjects in categories ranging from very good to very poor. Some clinical judgment on the part of the raters is involved in this process.

Although objective categorization is the clear-cut goal of the Harrow interview, subjectivity cannot altogether be avoided. When the subject is required to choose an answer, that answer must be interpreted within the personal parameters of the specific subject so that, to give one common example, verbal indication of a subject's deterioration in her housekeeping is interpreted as a sign of growth in a highly perfectionistic woman and as a sign of regression in a woman with a history of slovenliness.

The Rorschach Psychological Functioning Scale

The Rorschach Psychological Functioning Scale (RPFS), a sensitive measure of internal functioning, complements the measurement of external functioning by the Harrow interview. It focuses on two internal aspects that are regarded as components of normal, healthy adaptation: structural soundness and functional richness. Individuals with weak structures adjust poorly to the world—they are unable to perceive external reality in consensually validated terms, and lack control and balance in thought and feelings—while individuals weak in function adjust poorly to themselves. Persons in this latter group, unable to contact their own highly personalized

Table A–2
RPFS Functioning Levels

Score	Functioning Level Category
42 (very good)	Unimpaired functioning
40–41	Mildly impaired functioning
36–39	Moderately impaired functioning
30–35 (poor)	Severely impaired functioning
21–29	Barely able to function outside protected environment
20 and below	Unable to function outside of protected environment

internal worlds, are likely to behave in hollow conformity to perceived norms rather than to adapt meaningfully to the external world.

For my purposes, the six RPFS functioning levels were reduced to five in order to correspond with the five levels of separation in the Separation-Individuation Scale (SIS). The original six functioning levels, adapted from the ones used by Barbara Lerner in a 1972 study (see bibliography), are shown on table A-2.

The Separation-Individuation Scale (SIS)

Scoring Technicalities

Here is an addendum to the interpretation of Marie's response to card 4 (figure 4) that appears in chapter 7:

Intrinsic ambiguities in this story make it a difficult one to score. Although the subject idealizes people and sees them as undifferentiated, thereby fulfilling the first two criteria for level III, she also gives signs of personal interrelatedness and of accepting the nurturing role, the last two criteria for level V. The story falls somewhere in between the two levels. Further, the level V criteria are not completely fulfilled, and it is all but impossible to say with certainty whether nurturance and/or intimacy problems are resolved. Not enough detail is offered to clarify whether the clinging of the girl to the man denies separateness, reveals comfort with nurturing and intimacy (V.3 and V.4), or expresses a deep, primal need for contact that requires a clingy, dependent relationship (II.4)—or all of the above. (See level descriptions on pages 40 and 37.) This lack of clarity leads to a compromise scoring at level IV.

Instructions for Initial Telephone Contact

Begin by:

1. Asking casual questions, for example, how many children do you have? Are your parents living? If not, when did they die?
2. Screening for prior psychiatric hospitalizations
3. Paraphrasing cover letter which explains the purpose of the study. For example: "We are in the process of recruiting volunteers for research which deals with development in later life. This exploratory study focuses on women, with particular emphasis on how the parental woman adapts to later losses."

Say that:

1. The interview may prove to be an interesting experience or perhaps even a rewarding or integrative one (whether it will be depends on the sophistication of the subject)
2. A summary of the findings will be made available to the subject prior to submission of the study

Assure the prospective subject that all material is strictly confidential.

As a last resort if the prospective subject remains reluctant to participate, mail her a form describing the nature of the research in greater depth and follow this up with telephone call.

Instructions for Test Administration

To the interviewer:

1. Allow the subject to read and sign the consent form, if she has not already done so
2. Inform the subject that the checklist is routine and, though the questionnaire assesses a range of functioning from normal to problematic, the emphasis here is on normal functioning

To the tester:

1. General rules for the administration of tests
   a) To subjects with odd numbers (all subjects have numerical designations), administer tests in this order:
      (1) the Harrow Functioning Interview
      (2) the symptom checklist (self-administered)
      (3) the SIS test
      (4) the Rorschach
   b) Reverse the order of the SIS and Rorschach tests in testing even-numbered subjects
   c) Use the standard administration procedure, as outlined by Henry in *The Analysis of Fantasy* and by Beck in *Rorschach Test, I, Basic Processes* (see bibliography)
2. The Rorschach Test
   a) Ask the subject what she knows about this instrument without calling it a test)

b) Explain that the Rorschach is a tool used to understand people better and that it is not being used in this case for diagnostic purposes

c) If the subject is resistant, suggest that the Rorschach may uncover latent interests or capacities, for example, an ability to organize or a capacity for inner living, and that such information will be communicated to her; treat resistance casually and proceed to testing

d) Be sure not to prompt the subjects with leading questions about Rorschach or SIS images; allow free responses. It is best for the subjects to be naive about the purpose of the research, except as it is briefly described in the introductory remarks

e) Require at least two responses to each Rorschach card (suggest that "most people see more than one thing")

f) Record responses verbatim

3. SIS administration
   a) Show the SIS cards in this sequence: 2, 1, 4, 3, 5
   b) Introduce the cards like this: "I'd like you to make up a story about the people in the picture. What are they thinking and feeling, and what are the events that led up to the situation? How does it come out?"
   c) Allow the subjects to speak spontaneously, but limit them to five interpretations per card
   d) Record responses verbatim

4. Arrangements
   a) Arrange to administer the tests in the subjects' homes at times that are mutually convenient
   b) Refer problems regarding the arrangements or the proceedings to supervising investigators

5. Assessment
   a) Rate the subject's conduct at the end of the session. Since her capacity for intimacy may be revealed in her interactions with you, assess her need for control, her distance, and her cooperation, as well as the quality and appropriateness of affect as revealed through her body language
   b) Write a brief description of the subject's physical appearance. How did she present herself to you? Is she youthful, stylish, conservative, old fashioned?

6. Completion
   a) Check to make sure that you have completed all the tests and have filled in all the responses for which you are responsible
   b) Make sure that you also have a signed consent form and a completed symptom checklist from the subject

**Beyond Separation, or Postpartum Lines
of Research**

Other issues related to separation and loss invite serious study. Some specific questions in this field that I would like to see answered are described here.

1. Judith Ballou suggests that the mother deals with the loss of her childhood by identifying with her infant and enjoying care vicariously (see bibliography). Does becoming mature then mean giving up "symbiosis" in order to gain ever greater autonomy, while holding on to the loss through identification? It is possible to apply this conceptual framework to any developmental landmark in which separation and loss lead to greater differentiation, from the autonomy and separation of childhood and adolescence, to the growth of one's own children, to the ultimate loss of one's parents.

2. Helene Deutsch writes that a woman's conflicts over dependency issues may be revived when her child reaches the same developmental landmarks she has encountered (see bibliography). Assuming that she resolves some of the issues each time around, how is the potential for separation affected by the appearance (and by all the consequences thereof) of the first and of each subsequent child?

3. Other factors relevant to separation pertain to the duration of the mothering. How is the mother's view of herself and of her child affected by her experience of a miscarriage? of a baby's death? of the death of an older child?

4. The potential benefits of the mothering experience raise many as yet unanswered questions: Does the need to adapt to the changing needs and demands of children prepare mothers to handle later stresses better than childless women? Does pregnancy prepare them for later physical changes? Are narcissistic mothers immune to benefits other women derive from mothering?

5. The possibility that mothering per se has no benefit to the mother is also provocative. Do childless women surpass mothers in personal growth if they receive personal fulfillment through their social and professional achievements? Do these achievements actually gratify a "mothering need"? Are such childless women less ambivalent about their adult roles than mothers are?

6. And here is perhaps the most important question: Is separation as critical to adjustment as Mahler and others believed? Studying superficially well-functioning narcissists suggests that women can live fulfilling lives without separating, at least until their narcissistic supplies are depleted.

Bibliography

Abelin, Ernest L. "The Role of the Father in the Separation-Individuation Process." In, *Separation-Individuation*, edited by Margaret S. Mahler, 229–50. New York: International Universities Press, 1971.

Abramson, Jane B. *Evaluation of the Effects of Separation on Adaptation to Loss in Older Women Who Have Lost Their Mothers*. Ann Arbor, Mich.: University Microfilms International, 1985.

Ballou, Judith W. *The Influence of Object-Relational Paradigms on the Experience of Pregnancy and Early Motherhood*. Ann Arbor, Mich: University Microfilms International, 1975.

Beck, Samuel J. *Rorschach's Test I—Basic Processes*. New York: Grune & Stratton, 1961.

Benedek, Therese. "Parenthood as a Developmental Phase." *Journal of the American Psychoanalytic Association*, 7(1959):389–417.

Bettleheim, Bruno, quoted in Cardin, Marie, *The Words to Say It*. Cambridge: Van Vactor & Goodheart, 1983, 308.

Brusch, Hilde. *Eating Disorders*. New York: Basic Books, 1973, 69–70.

Deutsch, Helene, in Ballou, Judith W. *The Influence of Object-Relational Paradigms on the Experience of Pregnancy and Early Motherhood*. Ann Arbor, Mich: University Microfilms International, 1975.

Erikson, Erik H. *Childhood and Society*. New York: W.W. Norton, 1963.

Franklin, Girard. "The Quest for Certainty in Psychoanalytic Therapy." In *Psychologist-Psychoanalyst* 6(1985):4.

Grinker, Roy R., Sr. "The Borderline Syndrome: A Phenomenological View." In *Borderline Personality Disorders*, edited by Peter Hartocollis, 159–72. New York: International Universities Press, 1977.

Gunderson, John G., and Margaret T. Singer. "Defining Borderline Patients: An Overview." *American Journal of Psychiatry* 132(1975):1–10.

Gutmann, David. "The Clinical Psychology of Late Life: Developmental Paradigms." Paper presented at the West Virginia Gerontology Conference: Transitions in Aging, Morgantown, West Virginia, May 23–26, 1979.

Harrow, Martin, Evelyn Bromet, and Donald Quinlan. "Predictors of Post–hospital Adjustment in Schizophrenia." *The Journal of Nervous and Mental Disease* 58(1974):25–36.

Henry, William E. *The Analysis of Fantasy: The Thematic Apperception Technique in the Study of Personality.* New York: Robert E. Krieger, 1973.

Katz, Martin M. "Methods for Measuring Adjustment and Social Behavior in the Community." *Psychological Reports Monographs* 13(1963):503-35.

Kernberg, Otto F., quoted in Mahler, Margaret S., and Louise Kaplan, "Developmental Aspects in the Assessment of Narcissistic and So-called Borderline Personalities." In *Borderline Personality Disorders*, edited by Peter Hartocollis, 77. New York: International Universities Press, 1977.

Kernberg, Otto F. *Object Relations Theory and Clinical Psychoanalysis.* New York: Jason Aronson, 1976.

Kohut, Heinz. "The Disorders of the Self and Their Treatment." *International Journal of Psychoanalysis* 59(1978):413-25.

Lebe, Dorianne. "Individuation of Women." *Psychoanalytic Review* 69(1982):63-73.

Lerner, Barbara. *Therapy in the Ghetto.* Baltimore, Md.: Johns Hopkins University Press, 1972.

Lewis, Helen B. "Psychoanalysis as Therapy Today." In *Psychologist-Psychoanalyst* 6(1985-86):12-15.

Mahler, Margaret S. *The Psychological Birth of the Human Infant.* New York: Basic Books, 1975.

Mahler, Margaret S., and Louise Kaplan. "Developmental Aspects in the Assessment of Narcissistic and So-called Borderline Personalities." In *Borderline Personality Disorders*, edited by Peter Hartocollis, 73. New York: International Universities Press, 1977.

Parens, Henri. "Parenthood as a Developmental Phase." Panel report, *Journal of the American Psychoanalytic Association* 23(1975):154-65.

Vaillant, George E. *Adaptation to Life.* Boston: Little, Brown, 1974.

Winnicott, D.W. *The Maturational Process and the Facilitating Environment.* New York: International Universities Press, 1965.

Index

About the Author

Jane Abramson, Ph.D., was educated at Stanford University and at Sarah Lawrence College prior to receiving her doctorate in psychology from Northwestern University in 1984. Her areas of special training and interest include life-span developmental psychology, psychodiagnostics, the psychology of women, and psychoanalysis. Dr. Abramson has counseled individuals at both ends of the age spectrum and spent three years conducting the research for the present study, her first book.